HUSH MONEY

HUSH MONEY

How One Woman Proved Systemic Racism in her Workplace and Kept her Job

Inspired by True Events

Deborah Harris, Jacquie Abram, and Delilah Harris

ISBN: 9798554443305

Cover Design by: Bookcover_pro
Printed in the United States of America by Kindle Direct Publishing

This book is dedicated to our beautiful family member, Nita-Moe. Thank you for the love and excitement you showed as this book was being written, and for the hours of time you gave listening as each chapter was developed. We love you to the moon and back!

Contents

CHAPTER 1

Things Were Great in the Beginning

It was a chilly morning in the city of Austin, Texas on the day my life was changed. I was sitting at the dining table with mom, sipping a cup of coffee, and browsing the want ads in the newspaper as she read the headline news. Mom, a beautiful woman born in Shreveport, Louisiana, was fifty-one years old with a taller than average height, a slender physique, caramel-colored skin as smooth as silk, and glistening green eyes. She had long shiny black hair, dressed with a modest elegance, and had a personality that could charm a poisonous snake.

Mom adopted me when I was born and named me Ebony to highlight the beauty she saw in my dark skin. And although I didn't look anything like her, she was an amazing parent to me and was great in so many ways. The want ads, on the other hand, were not so great. Jobs that I was qualified for and that also paid well were far and few between, and I was tired of working dead-end jobs that made it hard to make ends meet.

As I wadded the want ads into a ball, Mom sensed my frustration, put down her newspaper, and placed her hand on top of mine.

"You can stay long as ya like, Ebony," she said, with love in her eyes. "But don't worry. God has a way of workin' things out."

Mom's words were encouraging, but it was her gentle touch that comforted me the most, and I was at a point in my life where I really needed comforting. At twenty-eight years old, I was going through a divorce, living with Mom in her small, one-bedroom apartment, and trying to get my son back from what was supposed to be a summer vacation in New York with his father.

As I thanked Mom for her support, the phone rang. It was a call from a woman at the temp agency I had signed up with two weeks earlier.

"Daebrun Career Institute needs a Secretary," she said. "It's a temp position that pays sixteen dollars and eighty-three cents an hour, the equivalent of thirty-five thousand dollars a year. Are you interested?"

Heck Yeah! That's a lot of mula! I thought to myself, before calmly verbalizing my interest.

And that's where my story begins, with the call that changed my life in the best way, and also the worst way. The call that began my six-figure career in higher education, and my descent into racial discrimination Hell.

When I hung up the phone, I was smiling from ear-to-ear and couldn't wait to share the good news with mom. Mom was thrilled.

"I told ya God has a way of workin' things out," she said. "All ya gotta do is believe."

The temp assignment wasn't a full-time job and didn't have any benefits. So, you're probably wondering why I was so excited. The reason is really quite simple. For the first time in my life I had gotten my foot in the door with a company that had *real* career potential. Daebrun Career Institute was a popular for-profit college with multiple campuses located in the United States, including several campuses in the State of Texas. I had seen Daebrun's commercials on television, and even considered enrolling in one of their degree programs. Working in higher education, even as a temp, was a step in the right direction as far as I was concerned.

In January 2012, my journey at Daebrun's main campus began in the same city where I lived, and from the very first day, it felt like home. Everything from the environment to the type of work I was doing was amazing. I was in perfect sync with the Chancellor, Dr. Hunter Hall, a professional, distinguished-looking man in his fifties, who exuded confidence and was as tall as a pro basketball player. He was a handsome man with tanned skin, fashionably styled salt and pepper hair, and an athletic physique. His eyes were greener than an emerald, and there was a warmth and kindness about him that immediately put me at ease.

Although Dr. Hall was the most powerful person on campus, he took me under his wing, and treated me much like the father figure I'd never had. I developed an instant respect for him and used the computer skills I taught myself at a safehouse for abused women to impress him. And impressed he was! He was amazed with my ability to manage budgets, prepare meeting minutes, and develop presentations, and he showed his appreciation every day. I enjoyed my job and planned to work for Dr. Hall and Daebrun for many years to come.

After working on my temp assignment for two months, Dr. Hall called me to his office to meet with him.

"You're the best assistant I've ever had," he said, with a smile. "And the only one that reminds me of a Nubian queen I saw in a movie yesterday."

"Thank you," I said, with a slight giggle. "It's my braids, isn't it?"

I had been styling my hair in dookie braids for the last two years because they were easy to do, and I always received so many compliments.

"Yes, it's your braids," he said, with a warm smile.

Then he said he was going to buy out my contract with the temp agency and hire me permanently.

"How does Senior Secretary sound?" He said, with a grin. "It comes with a five thousand dollar raise."

"That sounds amazing!" I exclaimed, as I jumped up and gave him a hug.

When I left his office, I was on top of the world and couldn't believe how quickly my hard work had paid off. In a matter of months, I had a full-time job that paid forty thousand dollars a year and came with excellent benefits including one hundred percent tuition reimbursement. I couldn't wait to tell Mom the good news, so I called her at work.

"Mom!" I exclaimed. "You'll never guess in a million years what happened!"

"You win the lotto child?"

"No, something better! Dr. Hall hired me full time and gave me a five thousand dollar raise!"

"I'm so proud of ya honey. God is good. I wish I could talk more, but gotta get back to them machines."

I could feel Mom's smile through the phone as she hung up and went back to work. Mom was a machinist and made eleven dollars an hour standing on her feet operating machines for ten hours a day, four days a week. Standing for that many hours a day would be hard for anyone, but for Mom it was especially hard because of her age and health issues. Now that I had a permanent job that paid well, my hope was that I could eventually take care of her, so she didn't have to work so hard.

Shortly after hanging up with mom, Dr. Hall called me back to his office.

"I want you to start managing my incoming email," he said. "I get too much, and there's not enough hours in the day to respond."

The next day, we met with the Director of Information Technology, and Dr. Hall instructed her to provide me with access to his email account, so I could manage it in a clandestine way. And even though she expressed concerns about providing me with access, she gave it to me anyway, and I began managing Dr. Hall's incoming email that day. I felt so important! I was privy to confidential, executive-level information, making important decisions on Dr. Hall's behalf, and doing my best to ensure that no one suspected that it was me, and not Dr. Hall, who was in control of his email account.

Things were great in the beginning, but then rumors began to spread throughout the campus that it was little ole' me, and not Dr. Hall, who was creating the responses coming from his email account. The rumors spread like wildfire and caused such an uproar that within days, dignitaries from Daebrun's parent company (Corporate) were at our campus interviewing employees. And when it was my turn to be interviewed, I was terrified! I felt like I was standing in front of a firing squad, both figuratively and literally.

"How long have you been pretending to be Dr. Hall?" A man asked.

"*What else* were you doing for Dr. Hall?" Another man rudely asked.

"Did you knowingly violate our IT Security policy?" A woman asked.

The questions came from left and right, and although I responded honestly, their stoic demeanor made me feel like Dr. Hall's job wasn't the only one at risk.

The Corporate reps continued grilling me for about an hour, and I was sweating bullets the whole time. Then, I was finally released. And as I walked back to my cubicle, all eyes were on me and I felt ashamed, even though I didn't think I had done anything wrong.

After what seemed like an eternity, Corporate emailed an organizational announcement to all staff and faculty stating that Dr. Hall had resigned from his position as Chancellor for personal reasons. When I received the email in my inbox, I was crushed because Dr. Hall was the best boss I'd ever had. And as I drove home, I experienced a rainbow of emotions: I was sad Dr. Hall was gone, happy I still had my job, worried about reporting to a new boss, and hopeful my future with Daebrun would still be bright.

Two weeks later, Mia Kelly, Dr. Hall's replacement as the new Chancellor, arrived on campus, and my hopes for a bright future at Daebrun were instantly dashed. Ms. Kelly was the polar opposite of Dr. Hall. She was a statuesque woman in her forties with cream-colored skin, shoulder-length, wavy, blonde hair, and vivid blue eyes that could melt the polar ice caps. She was as tall as a runway model, wore fitted dresses with high-heeled strappy sandals, and had a way of looking at me that sent chills down my spine.

Perhaps the biggest difference between Dr. Hall and Ms. Kelly was that Dr. Hall liked and respected me, and Ms. Kelly, on the other hand, despised me, and made sure I knew it during our first one-on-one meeting in her office.

"Listen, Agony," she said, with a low, sultry voice.

"Ebony, ma'am," I nervously replied, interrupting her. "My- my name is Ebony."

"Okay, *Ebony*, what are you, four feet tall?"

"No. I'm five-foot-four."

"Well, that's not tall enough, Agony. Wear higher heels. Towering over you makes my back hurt."

I'm a petite woman by nature and was already wearing two-inch high heels, so the idea that wearing higher heels would keep her from towering over me was laughable, and I did laugh because I thought she was joking. This was a mistake.

"Oh yes, I heard about you," she said, donning a wide smile as she stared at me. "*You're* the reason my predecessor is gone."

"That's not true," I declared, with eyes as big as saucers. "I don't know where this is coming from. Have I done something wrong?"

She didn't say a word. She just leaned back in her chair and continued staring at me like I was an alien she wanted to explore. I didn't know what to say or do, so I sat there speechless and awkwardly staring back. After two of the longest minutes I had ever experienced, she motioned me to leave, and I couldn't get out of there fast enough.

The next few months were particularly difficult as Ms. Kelly tried to break me, like I was a wild horse she was determined and eager to tame. She humiliated me in meetings on a daily basis, degraded and dehumanized me with threats and fear, took away the computer duties I enjoyed, and reduced my job to getting her coffee and running errands.

I'll never forget the day Ms. Kelly summoned me to her office where she was entertaining visitors from a sister campus. When I walked in, all eyes were locked on me, and I could tell I was the topic of much conversation.

"Meet Agony, my poor excuse for a Secretary," she said, as she flipped her hair back.

No one said a word, and the silence in the room was deafening. As everyone stared at me, I was frozen, too humiliated to move or even say what my correct name was. I just stood there like a deer caught in the headlights.

"Well, Agony? What are you waiting for?" She asked, raising her eyebrows at me. "Can't you see we need coffee?"

At that moment, I found just enough strength to turn around and walk out before bursting into tears. Then, I ducked into the bathroom and called mom.

"Sh- She's trying to break me," I said, in between sobs. "I don't know how much longer I can last."

"It breaks my heart to see ya hurtin' honey," Mom replied. "But don't make waves."

"What did I do to make her hate me so much?"

"You didn't do anything. We been dealing with this crap our whole lives. She don't want ya there 'cause your Black, but don't quit. Don't lose ya good job over this, okay?"

Mom could tell I was still distraught, so she left me with one final thought to ponder.

"I know it seems like she's in control, but I promise ya, it only seems that way. God's in control and He knows what ya going through."

Mom's reminder about God comforted me. So, after hanging up the phone, I asked God to give me strength, then went to the break room to make coffee. Afterwards, I took the cups of fresh coffee to Ms. Kelly's office, distributed them to each person, and quickly left.

When I returned to my cubicle, I decided to educate myself on workplace harassment because knowledge is power, and I needed to know if there was anything I could legally do to make it stop. I did some research and discovered that harassment, according to the Equal Employment Opportunity Commission, consists of unwelcome conduct based on a protected class such as race or skin color. It becomes illegal when the conduct is so severe and pervasive that it creates a work environment that is intimidating, hostile, or abusive.

Although Ms. Kelly had created a work environment that was intimidating, hostile, *and* abusive, the majority of her actions, from what I could tell, weren't based on a protected class and therefore were not illegal. And since I couldn't afford to quit my job, I continued reporting to her and suffering in silence for ten long months. That is, until the day she summoned me to her office for what I knew was to be fired. So, after taking my personal belongings to my car, I went to her office, sat down at her desk, and braced myself for the worst.

"Agony," she said, with a smug look on her face, "I hired a new Secretary. And since I don't need *two* Secretaries--"

"I know. I'm fired," I said, interrupting her train of thought. "I just don't know what I'm going to tell my son."

"Son?" She asked as her ears perked up. "You have a child?"

"Yes," I replied, as my eyes filled with tears. "I'm trying to save enough money to get him back from New York."

"Hmm, I didn't know that. You walk around here acting like everything is rainbows, bubble gum, and unicorns," she said.

I don't know if it was the knowledge that I was a mother, struggling financially, or had a son, that touched Ms. Kelly, but as I spoke, the smug look on her face disappeared before my eyes, and her icy heart seemed to thaw a little that day.

Then, she leaned back in her chair, crossed her toned legs, and sighed. "Ebony, you're not fired," she said. "We have an opening in the Student Finance department. If you want to transfer, we'll see how you do. It's a demotion, and your salary will be reduced, but if you want it, it's yours."

I don't know what shocked me more, that I still had a job, or that she finally said my name right, but as I sat there, tears began rolling down my cheeks as I silently cried.

When I left her office, I went back to my cubicle and thanked God that I still had my job, because I was still making more money than I had made in previous jobs, even with the reduced salary. The next day, I transferred to the Student Finance department where I was the only Black employee, my annual salary was reduced to thirty-seven thousand dollars, and my title was changed to Student Finance Advisor. As I sat in my new office and reflected on my first year of employment, I could hardly believe how fast my dream job turned into a nightmare simply because there was a change in leadership from a great boss to a horrific one. But now that I no longer reported to Ms. Kelly, I was confident there would be nothing but sunshine and blue skies ahead of my career…or so I thought.

CHAPTER 2

From Victim to Outcast

In April 2013, my career as a Student Finance Advisor officially began. Since I had no experience, I was required to complete one week of rigorous training on everything there was to know about student finance, and one week shadowing other Student Finance Advisors as they met with students, during appointments, and completed their packaging. Packaging was a fancy word student finance professionals used to refer to the process of awarding financial aid, consisting of federal and state grants, federal student loans, scholarships and other sources of aid, to eligible students.

It was during the shadowing phase that I realized how inconsistent the appointments were from person to person, and how manual their processes were, especially the process of calculating how much financial aid a student was eligible to receive. Day after day, I shadowed other Student Finance Advisors and watched in horror as they manually calculated everything from the total cost of tuition, books, and fees, to the total amount of financial aid each student was eligible to receive. And every time, without fail, they accidently input the wrong number into the calculator and was forced to redo the calculation. These errors caused the appointment to drag on for way too long and put a bad taste in the mouth of the frustrated student.

Determined not to suffer the same fate, I used my computer skills to create an electronic version of the direct cost sheet my teammates were using, and added formulas to automate the process. When I used it during my first appointment with a student, instead of the manual cost sheet my teammates were using, it calculated everything correctly within seconds, reduced the appointment time by a whopping thirty-minutes, and really impressed my manager who was observing the appointment. The next day, at my manager's request, I trained everyone in the department on how to utilize the electronic version I created, and it became the standard for calculating eligibility from that day forward.

Meeting with students brought me unexpected joy because I realized that many of them were just like me: Raised in poverty as children, remained in poverty as adults, and hopeful that earning a degree would improve their circumstances. These commonalities fueled my passion for providing each student with outstanding customer service, and I quickly became a favorite in the Student Finance department. On any given day, you could hear students in the hallway singing my praises to their friends, or recommending me as a point of contact, and it wasn't long before Ms. Kelly took notice and decided to capitalize on it.

"I've scheduled a photoshoot for the campus, and you need to participate," she said, with a big smile on her face. "Our students love you, and you're basically a celebrity here."

The following week, a marketing team came to the campus and took professional photos of me interacting with other staff members selected by Ms. Kelly. For many hours that day, I worked with coworkers who pretended to be students in various scenarios, and it was a fun experience. A week later, Ms. Kelly took out ads containing photos of me in a local magazine, and even scheduled interviews of me with the magazine's reporters. I have to admit, I loved the attention I was getting, even though Ms. Kelly really pushed the black factor.

Ms. Kelly paid extra to expedite things and two weeks later, there were photos of me in the school catalog, on free promotional swag, and on posters hanging in the hallways. My face was everywhere, and because of my interviews in the local magazine, Daebrun saw an increase in minority enrollments.

I can't be sure what the motivating factor was, but a few weeks later, Ms. Kelly transferred Latoya Johnson to the Student Finance department, and told me to personally train her. Latoya was a pregnant woman in her twenties with an average height, mahogany skin she slathered with cocoa butter to prevent stretch marks, and hypnotic gray eyes she said came from her mother. She had chestnut brown hair that flowed down her back, a larger-than-life personality, and a reputation for being ghetto fabulous.

"Are you the trainer for our department or somethin'?" Latoya asked, as she rubbed a mountain of cocoa butter on her arms. "Girl, I don't mean to be rude, but some of these folks said you're just as new as I am. So, isn't that like the blind leadin' the blind?"

"Ms. Kelly told me to train you," I replied. "That's all I know."

"Nuff said," Latoya declared.

Although our personalities were quite different, we had three things in common: We were both Christians, we were both hard workers, and we were both Black. Our commonalities made working together easy, and I was happy to no longer be the only Black person on the team.

Over the next two years, I used my computers skills to help my manager improve operations, identify past due cash, develop a strategy to complete packages timely, and create a presentation to standardize the information communicated to students.

Because of my hard work and efforts, I became an informal team lead, and my career was finally back on track. That is, until February 2015, when Ms. Kelly demoted my manager, and hired a man by the name of Malcolm Webb as the Associate Director of Student Finance. Malcolm was a professionally laid-back man in his thirties with ivory skin, a stocky build, and shoulder-length brown hair slicked back into a low ponytail. He had hazel eyes, wore gold stud earrings in both ears, and had a blinding smile with the whitest teeth I'd ever seen.

On his first day as our new supervisor, Malcolm called a team meeting in the conference room, and asked everyone to introduce themselves one at a time. One by one, each person stated their name, how long they had been working for Daebrun, and one fun fact. When it was my turn to speak, I said, "My name is Ebony. I've been working at Daebrun for almost three years, and I like playing scary video games."

"I like your name, Ebony," Malcolm said, with a smile and a deep, raspy voice. "It suits you well."

"Thank you, I think so, too."

"I'm also intrigued by the way you speak. How did you learn to speak so articulately?"

"When I was seven years old, I watched TV for hours with my mom, everything from reporters on the news to prime-time soap operas, after I finished my homework. Then, I pretended to be the characters I saw as I played with mom. For years, I thought we were just playing a fun game, but when I got older, I realized Mom used the characters on TV to teach me how to effectively communicate."

"Wow, what an amazing story. Thanks for sharing."

Malcolm seemed like a nice man, and was a seasoned student finance professional with many years of experience under his belt. And, initially, I was excited to learn under his leadership. It became apparent very quickly, though, that he didn't share my enthusiasm.

Right from the start, Latoya and I noticed that Malcolm treated us differently than others in our department. It started out with small things like excluding us from lunch gatherings and offering snacks to everyone except us. But then he started holding team meetings without us, and requiring us to constantly work the late shift while everyone else went home on time.

One day, I poked my head into his office where he was working at his desk.

"Do you have a moment?" I politely asked.

"Not really," he replied, avoiding eye contact with me. "What do you need?"

"I was wondering if it's possible to have team meetings that include everyone, so we can all be on the same page," I said. "Latoya and I feel like we're missing important information being shared with others."

"You don't say!" he said, with a chuckle. "Here's the deal, Ebony. *If* there's something I feel you need to know, I'll be the first one to tell you. Anything else?"

"No, that was it."

There was an awkward silence for several seconds as he stared at me, and I stared back at him. Disappointed, I turned and walked away, and could feel his hazel eyes burning a hole in the back of my head until I exited his office.

Afterwards, I pulled Latoya aside and told her what happened.

"He's obviously a racist," I said.

"No," she said, shaking her head. "Maybe he got issues with you *questionin'* his authority, and I don't want no part a whatever's goin' on in that head of yours."

I could tell I was making Latoya nervous, and didn't want to press the issue or alienate her in any way. So, I dropped it and we both went back to work. But try as I might, I couldn't get my concerns about Malcolm

12

being a racist out of my mind for the rest of the day, and most of the night.

The next morning, I pulled Latoya aside again.

"Toy, he's discriminating against us plain and simple, and it's gonna get worse if we don't do something. Do you think we should complain to Ms. Kelly?"

"Oh, Hell-l-l no!" Latoya exclaimed, all fired up. "That's a great way to get fired and ain't nobody got time for that! Complainin' is White people shit. And anyway, we don't have no proof!"

"But we do have proof!" I said, passionately. "He's openly treating us different! Anyone who--"

"Stop, girl! Damn!" Latoya said, forcefully interrupting me. "Even if he is discriminatin' against us, at least we still have jobs. Ms. Kelly will fire us both if we complain."

I paused for a moment to collect my thoughts because I knew she was right. Then I calmly explained that I read our anti-discrimination policy, and it said employees can report discrimination anonymously by calling Corporate's confidential hotline and leaving a message. According to the policy, once it's reported, Corporate will conduct an investigation, and Ms. Kelly will never know who submitted the complaint because the information will be kept strictly confidential.

After thinking about it for a minute, Latoya nodded her head and sighed.

"Okay, girl, this could work, but I ain't making the call," she said.

"No worries," I replied. "I'll make the call tonight."

When I got home, Mom was sitting at the dining table mixing a cup of baking soda water.

"Hey honey, how was ya day?" She asked, looking at me with dark circles under her eyes, and sounding a little tired.

"Long. I'm glad to be home. You feeling ok, mom?"

"I'm constipated and my stomach's upset. Must've ate somethin' bad."

Then, Mom chugged the baking soda water down, kissed me on the forehead, and went off to bed.

I wasn't planning to keep Mom in the dark about what I intended to do, but decided at the last minute not to tell her. It would only make her worry, and she needed to rest. So, after verifying that Mom was asleep, I made the phone call to the anonymous hotline using my best fake accent to disguise my voice.

"I'm an employee at the main campus. I'd like to file a complaint against Malcolm Webb, the Associate Director of Student Finance. He's discriminating against his negros. He's excluding them negro folks from meetings and lunches, sharin' his snacks with everyone else, and forcin' em to work late while everyone else gets to leave on-time. I hope y'all will investigate."

As I hung up the phone, I felt good knowing I had done the right thing, and confident that all would be well.

Now, hindsight is 2020, and looking back, reporting discrimination anonymously was *absolutely* the wrong thing to do, because Corporate didn't conduct the investigation themselves like the policy said they would. Instead, they notified Ms. Kelly that an anonymous discrimination complaint was received, and instructed *her* to investigate it. And since it was more important to her to find out who the rat was than to actually conduct an investigation, she used the process of elimination to flush out the guilty party.

She started with Latoya. My heart raced as I watched Ms. Kelly go into Latoya's office and walk away with her in tow. About twenty-five minutes later, Latoya walked back to her office with Ms. Kelly following close behind her, and when her teary eyes met mine as I intensely watched from my office, she mouthed the words *"I'm sorry"*. When I read her lips, my heart sank into my stomach, and I felt violently ill.

Then, Ms. Kelly went into Malcolm's office and closed the door behind her. For the next twenty minutes, I sat in my office on the verge of vomiting, and wishing I was a fly on the wall in Malcolm's office.

When Ms. Kelly finally came out, she made her way to my desk, and if looks could kill, I would've been dead in my chair.

"Ebony, a word?" She said, with a low growl as she turned and walked away.

I slowly stood up and began following her, and as I walked, there was no doubt in my mind, I was in deep, deep trouble.

When we arrived at Ms. Kelly's office and walked in, she closed the door behind us, and tore into me like a rabid dog before I even had a chance to sit down.

"After everything I've done for you! After everything I gave you! You air our dirty laundry to Corporate? I made you a celebrity! I gave you a career, and this is how you repay me? I should've fired you when I had the chance!"

"I-I'm sorry, Ms. Kelly," I replied, as my eyes welled up with tears.

"Oh, you're sorry alright!" She snarled. "Sorriest excuse for an employee I've ever seen! And you've committed career suicide. So, think about that, and get out of my office!"

Tears flowed freely from my eyes as I left her office and began the long walk of shame back to mine. And as I got closer to the Student Finance department, I saw Malcolm, standing in the entryway, and grinning at me like an evil clown in a horror movie. I was emotionally exhausted after the verbal beating I took from Ms. Kelly, so I scurried passed him, went into my office and closed the door, and breathed a sigh of relief because I still had my job, and hoped everything would blow over and return to normal in a few days.

When I arrived at work the next day, I realized that everything *was not* going to blow over and return to normal anytime soon. Malcolm was furious when Ms. Kelly informed him that I made the anonymous phone call to Corporate. So, he retaliated against me. He reviewed my completed work and riddled it with errors making it appear that I was incompetent and putting my job at risk, verbally abused me in front of coworkers, called me Darky in private, and made me work more late shifts than anyone else. And, since he knew my sister was now a student at Daebrun, he tampered with her financial aid which caused a delay in the additional student loan funds she had borrowed to help Mom catch up on her car payments, which delayed the stipend check she was supposed to receive, and resulted in mom's car being repossessed.

Things with Malcolm were so bad that I dreaded coming to work, afraid of the new attacks each day would bring. My job became a living nightmare from which I could not awake, gave me an enormous amount of anxiety, and resulted in forty pounds of weight gain over a three-month period due to stress.

One afternoon, Malcolm stopped by my office unexpectedly, and closed the door.

"My how the mighty have fallen," he said, with a light-hearted chuckle. "The posters of you were pulled down a few minutes ago, and

15

your face is being removed from *all* marketing material as we speak. So, guess what? No more celebrity Ebony!"

Then, he shrugged his shoulders and cheerfully said, "Oh well. Ready to quit yet Darky?"

I didn't say a word, I just stared at my computer screen, and feverishly typed while he stood in front of my desk glaring at me in a way that gave me the creeps. He glared at me for about a minute and then, out of nowhere, busted out laughing. He laughed so hard he almost choked on his own spit.

As he stood in front of my desk pointing at me and laughing, I wanted to cry, but managed to hold the tears back long enough for him to get the hell out of my office. Then, I cried. I felt so alone, and there was no one I could turn to for help, because Ms. Kelly retaliated against me, too. She spread vicious rumors about me across the campus and labeled me as the girl who cried racism. And because she was the Chancellor, and her words carried a huge amount of weight, she transformed me from the racial discrimination victim that I was into a social outcast, and no one, not even Latoya, wanted to talk to me let alone be seen with me. And I didn't dare file another discrimination complaint. I was too afraid of being fired or making matters worse.

As I sat at my desk crying, I knew it was just a matter of time before Malcolm unjustly fired me, or I buckled under the pressure of his hate and resigned. I also knew that no matter which method brought about the loss of my job, the end result would still be the same. Without my job, I would go spiraling back into poverty, and the thought terrified me.

As I continued worrying about my job, my mind began to wander, and I started having dark thoughts, very dark thoughts, about Malcolm, and what I would do if I ever saw him alone in a dark alley with no cameras and no witnesses. I'd do my best to beat the living shit out of him, stab him a few times with a butcher knife, then force feed him *my* shit until he gagged and begged for mercy. And if he tried to crawl away as he bled, I'd pull out my gun and shoot him. Yeah, just shoot him. Or should I stab him again? Stab him or shoot him? Shoot him or stab him? Stab him or shoot him...

For the next fifteen minutes, I sat at my desk smiling, blankly staring at the wall, as I embraced the darkness and imagined all the ways I would hurt and kill Malcolm. Suddenly, the phone on my desk rang, snapping me back to reality. I was alarmed by my desires, especially because I began to understand the conditions that cause good people to snap, hunt down, and kill their bosses, along with anyone else who gets in the way. So, I quickly grabbed my keys and purse and left the place fostering my evil thoughts. And as I drove out of the parking lot, and reflected back on the last three years of my employment, I assured myself that there *was* a light at the end of the dark tunnel, even though I couldn't see it yet, and it wasn't a freight train coming to run me down…or so I thought.

CHAPTER 3

Escaping the Carnival of Horrors

By the time I made it home from work, I was mentally and emotionally drained. I wanted to go to sleep but couldn't bear the thought of sleeping on mom's uncomfortable couch another night, especially after the dreadful day I had.

Mom's bedroom wasn't necessarily big, but she had a king-size bed that was quite comfy, and since she slept alone, there was plenty of room on the other side. So, I dragged my tired butt to mom's room where she was sleeping.

"Mom? Mom? Can I sleep with you?" I whispered, as I leaned over her head. "I had a really bad day."

Mom awoke just long enough to nod her head a couple of times, and a few seconds later, she was sound asleep again.

I walked around the bed to the other side, sat down on the edge, and stared through the moonlit room at the painting of three palm trees hanging on the wall, in an attempt to calm my spirit. But try as I might, I couldn't get the dark thoughts I was having about Malcolm to abate, and I felt the evil taking root in the deepest, darkest corners of my soul. I was in spiritual agony, as I struggled to resist the darkness and stay in the light, and with nowhere else to turn, I dropped to my knees, closed my eyes as tears rolled down both cheeks, and sought help from the last person I considered asking to come to my aid.

"Mom's been telling me about you my whole life," I softly prayed, "and I always pray to God in your name because that's what I was taught to do. But if you're real, please come into my heart and help me. Amen."

I knew it was a simple prayer, but if Mom was right about everything she taught me over the years, I knew that Jesus would hear my prayer no matter how simple it was.

After praying, I climbed into mom's bed, laid my head on the pillow, and blankly stared at the doorway as my eyes became heavy, and I began to fall asleep. Now, I don't know if I was dreaming, or if I was half asleep and half awake, but as I laid there completely relaxed, and with eyelids more than half closed, I saw a beautiful, royal blue scarf floating in slow motion through the doorway into mom's room. It was incredibly long, sparkled all over like it was covered in diamonds, and floated in the shape of a winding river moving side to side, this way and that way.

When the scarf reached the foot of the bed, it began wrapping around me, starting at my feet, and moving upward. When the tip reached my face, I felt a lightness inside my heart, and an energy that can only be described as unworldly, radiating from the scarf. And when I heard the gentle voice of a man who I instinctively knew was Jesus say, "I love you, and am with you", a peace came over me, and my spirit was finally at ease.

Suddenly, I was fully awake, and overcome with joy and emotion. So, I jumped up and with tears running down my face, woke Mom and told her about everything I had been dealing with at work, including Ms. Kelly's harassment, Malcolm's discrimination and retaliation, the evil thoughts that had taken over my mind, and the amazing experience I had with Jesus. Mom was emotional.

"Oh, honey, you don't fight evil with evil," she cried, as she grabbed my hand. "When someone's doing evil against ya or doing ya harm, Jesus is the first person ya ask for help, not the last, okay?"

"Okay, mom."

Afterwards, we both fell fast asleep, and from that day forward, I slept with Mom every night, and knew I could face whatever came next because Jesus was with me.

The next day, I went back to work, where Malcolm continued tormenting me for weeks on end and trying to force me to resign. That is, until the day Ms. Kelly went on vacation, and I saw a glorious ray of sunlight at the end of the dark tunnel I had been stuck in for far too long. The sunlight was in the form of a call I received from one of Daebrun's National Directors. National directors were one level higher than campus directors and staff in the organizational hierarchy, because they were responsible for providing training, oversight, and resources to all campuses in the Daebrun division. Although National directors were located at the Austin campus, their offices were in a building completely separate from campus staff, faculty, and students.

When I answered the call, Amanda Ross, the National Director of Human Resources, instructed me to come to her office immediately. Amanda was a full-figured woman in her mid-forties with a rosy complexion, amber eyes as bright as the sun, and shoulder-length brown hair with a side bang. She had a pair of reading glasses sitting on top of her head, wore designer suits and flats, and had more diamonds on her fingers, ears, neck, and wrists than my jewelry collector friend had in stock.

When I arrived at Amanda's office, walked in, and saw Kyle Charron, the National Director of Student Finance, alarms went off in my head and I feared I was about to be fired. Kyle was a tall, lanky man in his fifties with a personality that left a lot to be desired. He had a freckled complexion, olive green eyes, and military cut, ginger red hair. He wore rectangle wire frame glasses on the tip of his nose, called himself a good ole' country boy, and had a way of speaking that rendered most people powerless to respond.

After exchanging pleasantries, I sat down and waited for one of them to tell me that my services were no longer needed. While I waited, I discreetly counted the personal items I wanted to get from my office in my head, so I could make a quick getaway when it was over and spare myself some embarrassment. Finally, Kyle spoke, breaking the silence.

"The SF Director in Temple quit yesterday," he said, with a strong twang. "That S.O.B. left us in a hot mess on a cold night, and we're not hiring' another snake in the grass to hem haw around and jack things up."

At this point, I was thoroughly confused, not only by the way he talked, but also because I literally had no idea why he was speaking with me about problems at the Temple campus.

"Folks 'round here say you're a problem solver and have a fire in your belly that's not gas, young lady." Kyle continued. "So, I'm taken a chance, and recommending you for the position."

When I heard him say he was recommending me for what I assumed was a promotion, I swallowed the wrong way, almost choked on the mint in my mouth, and started coughing non-stop. Thankfully, Amanda jumped into the conversation, giving me a few extra moments to regain my composure.

"If you're interested," she said, twirling the eighteen-carat diamond ring on her finger. "I'll set up the interview with Dr. Romano, the Chancellor in Temple. She's excited to meet you."

I wanted to jump for joy but was skeptical because Ms. Kelly said I had committed career suicide when I filed the anonymous discrimination complaint.

"Does Ms. Kelly know about this?" I asked, squinting my eyes to block the brilliance of her diamonds.

"Mia is on vacation and *I'm* acting Chancellor," Amanda said, sounding annoyed. "So, the decision is mine to make. I support moving forward if you want this opportunity."

After thanking them both and confirming my interest, I left Amanda's office in complete shock. Ms. Kelly said I had committed career suicide, but my career was still alive, and a promotion was within my reach!

When I returned to my office, I called Mom and shared the amazing news with her.

"Thank ya, Jesus! That's wonderful news!" She exclaimed. "You'll do great in the interview, honey. You were blessed with the gift of gab."

The following week, I drove to the Temple campus, an hour commute from Austin, to meet with the Chancellor, Dr. Sofie Romano. Dr. Romano was a woman in her early fifties with an average height and build, skin the color of warm sand, brown boyish cut hair, and soulful brown eyes. She wore tailored pants suits, masculine dress shoes, and no jewelry except a photo necklace with a picture of her wife.

The interview went very well, and Dr. Romano was so impressed that she hired me on the spot as the new Director of Student Finance (a level one step higher than Malcolm's position in the organizational hierarchy). She also offered me a salary of fifty-five thousand dollars per year. I was elated! In three years' time, my salary jumped from thirty-five thousand dollars a year to fifty-five thousand dollars, I was the leader of the Student Finance department in Temple, and, best of all, I had found a way to escape from Malcolm's carnival of horrors!

In July 2015, I transferred to the Temple campus where I was the only Black employee in a management position. I planned to call a quick team meeting to spend a little time getting to know my two employees. But before I had a chance, one of my employees popped his head into my office.

"Welcome aboard, Ms. Ebony!" He exclaimed, as he walked in, invited himself to have a seat in one of the chairs in front of my desk, and crossed his legs in comfort. "Sorry for barging in, just wanted to introduce myself. I'm Michael."

Michael Sullivan was a man in his twenties and was the newest member of my team. Although he had an average height, he was dashingly handsome with tanned skin, butter blonde hair, deep blue eyes, and a sculpted body. He exuded sex appeal as if he carried pheromones in his pocket, thought highly of himself both professionally and physically, and believed he was the best thing to come into the world since the invention of chocolate.

"No worries, Michael. It's nice to meet you."

"I know it is," he said, with a light laugh as he leaned back. "You can look, but no touchy touchy. Just kidding."

Oh brother, I thought to myself. *This one's going to be a handful.*

"How long have you been working here, Michael?" I asked.

"Six months, but I know everything about student finance, so feel free to come to me if you need help."

"I will keep that in mind. Thanks for stopping by."

And with that, he walked out of my office, and I was left wondering if he was on something.

After meeting Michael, I thought it only fair to spend some time getting to know my other employee, Marisol Gutierrez, so I called her, and invited her to come to my office. When she walked in and sat down, I began to wonder if I was running the Student Finance department or a modeling agency. Marisol, like Michael, was attractive and was the only employee in my department who spoke and understood Spanish. She was a petite woman in her twenties with long, jet black hair, doe-shaped brown eyes, long black lashes, and a "bangin' body" according to a student I overheard in the hallway. She wore fitted dresses to accentuate her curves, had a delightful personality, and it was easy to see why students and staff alike enjoyed interacting with her.

"It's nice to meet you, Marisol." I said. "I've heard great things about you."

"Thanks, boss. I'm happy you're here."

"How long have you been working here?"

"Five years. Everyone comes and goes, but me--I stay 'cause I like my job."

After Marisol left my office, I received a phone call. It was Kyle Charron, the National Director of Student Finance who recommended me for the promotion.

"I know you don't have management experience, young lady, but don't fret none 'cause I'm sending someone to train you."

"I won't fret none. At least not until I figure out what fret none is."

Kyle laughed in amusement at my response, then said he arranged for Malcolm, my racist tormentor at the Austin campus, to provide me with the management training I needed, instead of doing it himself. Disturbing, right?

The next day, Malcolm arrived at the Temple campus and immediately started talking shit.

"Come back to Austin, Ebony," he said, with a laugh as he adjusted his ponytail. "We both know you don't have what it takes to run this office."

When Malcolm was my boss, I was forced to bite my tongue so often that I started to taste blood. But now I was in a position higher than his, and wanted to finally give him a dose of his own medicine.

"I *do* have what it takes," I said, with a cheerful smile. "Afterall, I'm a director now, and you're *just an associate director*, right?"

I really should've followed mom's advice about not fighting evil with evil, and taken the high road, because although it felt great to get under Malcolm's skin, there was an unexpected consequence.

"Okay Darky, er, uh, Ebony," he said, making a Freudian slip as his face turned beet red. "I'll give you one day of training. That's it. One day. Then, you're on your own."

Then, over the next six hours, Malcolm rushed me through his so-called training so fast it made my head spin. And at the end of the day when he left, I was glad he took his toxic energy with him.

The next day, I proudly updated the title on my email signature line to Director of Student Finance, and then requested five hundred thousand dollars in past due federal funds, one of the primary functions Malcolm trained me to do. It was my understanding that the funds I requested would be deposited into the Temple bank account within two days.

Four days later, the funds I requested had not been received, and leaders at the campus, National, and Corporate levels were very concerned. And when Dr. Romano summoned me to her office to meet with her regarding the delay, she was none-to-pleased, and my job was off to a very rocky start.

"Ebony, I'm getting pressure from all directions! You said the funds would be here two days ago. *Where's the money?*"

"I'm working on it, Dr. R, but I honestly don't know what happened. I followed Malcolm's instructions to the letter."

"Then I suggest you call him and find out how to fix this thing!"

The disappointment in Dr. Romano's voice cut me like a knife because I knew I had let her down, and she was worried she had unwittingly hired another "snake in the grass" as Kyle so eloquently put it.

As I made my way back to my office, I was shaking my head in disgust. Malcolm intentionally trained me the wrong way on Requesting Federal Funds, a function, mind you, that he had been performing correctly since the day he was hired. And although Dr. Romano urged me to call him, I knew nothing good would come of it. He set me up to fail, and was probably sitting in his office laughing himself into hysteria.

When I got back to my office, I closed the door, sat down, and took a deep breath as I tried to figure out how to fix the mess I was in. Suddenly, my desk phone rang. It was Kyle Charron, the National Director of Student Finance.

"You got my knickers bunched up in all kinds of knots, young lady," he sharply said, with even more twang than I had previously remembered. "Where's the federal funds for your campus?"

"I requested them four days ago, but they never came in," I replied, sounding panicked and on the verge of tears. "Can you help me figure out what went wrong? I think Malcolm intentionally trained me the wrong way and--"

"I'm fixing' to get upset and don't wanna hear no excuses," Kyle continued. "I took a chance on you without management experience against my better judgment, but if you can't do this job, I'll find someone who can." Then, he hung up on me.

After speaking with Kyle, I realized I was on my own, and if I was going to have any chance of being successful, I needed to figure out how to manage the Student Finance department myself. So, over the next two months, I worked fourteen-hour days, seven days a week, reading every technical manual published by the U.S. Department of Education, taking every online training course offered by student finance associations, developing important contacts in the industry with expertise in student finance management, and gaining detailed knowledge of student finance operations. And by the time I was finished, I had not only learned the correct way to Request Federal Funds, but had also acquired valuable knowledge that I used to develop new processes, retrain my staff, and successfully resolve every issue that had plagued my department for years, much to Dr. Romano's delight.

One day, Michael Sullivan stopped by my office.

"Can I talk to you, Ms. Ebony?"

"Sure."

Michael closed the door and sat down in front of my desk.

"Just wanted to say how great it is having you here," he said. "I mean, everyone looked down on us before 'cause we were so far behind, but now we're killing it, thanks to you."

"Thanks, Michael, but it wasn't just me," I replied. "You guys rock!"

"But I'm the greatest, right?" He said, eagerly awaiting my response.

I didn't say a word. I just stared at him, blinking several times.

"Just kidding," he replied, with a laugh.

One thing about Michael. He was always fishing for compliments about his looks or his skills. And although I never took the bait, I enjoyed having him on the team because he was a very hard worker who was ambitious and eager to learn. And even though he frequently got on my nerves with his arrogant nature, I trusted him, and knew I could rely on him to get things done.

Since my department was now running better than ever, in September 2015, I enrolled as a student at the Temple campus, even though I lived in Austin, and began pursuing a bachelor's degree in finance. My reasons for enrolling in Temple instead of Austin were two-fold: First, it was easier to attend class at the campus where I physically worked; and second, I didn't want Malcolm overseeing my financial aid because if anyone was a snake in the grass, it was Malcolm.

After I started attending classes at the Temple campus, I applied for financial aid, and requested to borrow additional student loan funds, just like my sister did, to help Mom buy a new car since her old car had been repossessed. Four days later, my desk phone rang. It was Miguel Vigil, the National Director of Accounting. Miguel was a strappingly handsome man in his late thirties with a taller than average height. He had olive colored skin, hair and eyes as dark as black sapphire, and a way of rolling his Rs that made most women, including me, weak in the knees.

"Good morning, Ebony. This is Miguel from Accounting. Is this a good time to talk?"

"Yes, it is. How can I help you?"

"Loan funds for a student at your campus were deposited into the Temple bank account today. An hour later, the deposit was canceled by Malcolm Webb at the Austin campus, and the funds were returned to the lender. Did you authorize Malcolm to initiate refunds for your campus?"

"Absolutely not," I replied. "Malcolm doesn't have *any* responsibilities for Temple. What's the student's name?"

Miguel was silent for several seconds, and I got a bad feeling in my gut.

"Umm, you are the student. Malcolm canceled your student loans and returned them to the lender."

When I heard this news, I was outraged! Then I asked Miguel to provide me with more details. Miguel said that Malcolm sent an email to Latoya Johnson, my ghetto fabulous ex-coworker at the Austin campus, instructing her to cancel the loan funds for the student named on the deposit roster that was attached to his email. When Latoya read the roster and saw my name, she hoped Malcolm had made an error. But when she brought it to his attention, he reprimanded her for questioning his authority, and required her to complete the task. Afterwards, she went to Miguel for help because she was concerned about being put in the middle of a feud between Malcolm and me.

Words cannot express how angry I was! Malcolm was still discriminating against me, but now he was doing it from a distance! •

After thanking Miguel for his call, I hung up and immediately called mom. I was overwhelmed and needed to hear the voice of reason.

"He's doing it again, mom!"

"Who's doin' what again?"

"Malcolm, mom! Malcolm!"

"But I thought he wasn't your manager anymore."

"He's not, but he's still after me!"

"Calm down honey, it's gonna be alright," Mom replied. "While he's diggin' a hole under you, he don't know God's diggin' a bigger hole under him. I guarantee you he'll fall in his hole before he finishes diggin' yours."

Normally, mom's words comforted me, but after hanging up, I was still terribly upset, and started dialing the number for Amanda Ross, the diamond-covered National Director of Human Resources at the Austin campus. In the middle of dialing, I was interrupted by Dr. Romano, who had poked her head into my office.

"My wife and I are going to lunch now," she said, standing in the doorway with both hands in her pants pockets. "Want us to bring you something back?"

"No, thank you," I said, with a shaky voice as I looked down at the papers on my desk.

"Are you okay?" She asked, walking in, and closing the door behind her.

"No. I'm being discriminated against by someone at the Austin campus. I'm calling Amanda Ross now to file a formal complaint."

Dr. Romano sat down in one of the chairs in front of my desk.

"I'm sorry to hear that," she said. "Let's call her together. I want to know what's going on as well."

I dialed Amanda on speaker phone and when she answered, I explained everything that Miguel had shared with me.

"If I'm understanding correctly, you think Malcolm canceled your loans for nefarious reasons, right?" She asked.

"Yes, that's correct," I replied.

"I'd be willing to bet my diamond necklace and my diamond ring on this being just a simple misunderstanding."

Amanda then wanted to know the reason I believed Malcolm's actions were less than honorable, so I explained to her that this was the second time he used financial aid as a tool to discriminate against me.

"The first time it happened," I explained, "he tampered with my sister's financial aid to indirectly discriminate against me, but I was too afraid to report it."

"These are serious allegations, and I understand your concern," Amanda replied. "We'll initiate a good faith investigation, and notify you when it's complete."

When I hung up, I felt an undeniable sense of relief in knowing that a good faith investigation would be conducted, and was confident that when the investigation was complete, Malcolm would be reprimanded or possibly even fired, and the discrimination would cease. I also had a good feeling about Amanda. She empathized with me, something I didn't expect from someone so wealthy, and gave me hope. And although I didn't know what a good faith investigation entailed, I had no reason to distrust her…or so I thought.

CHAPTER 4

The 'E' in Email Stands for Evidence

One month had passed since I spoke with Amanda Ross, the National Director of Human Resources, and made my discrimination complaint against Malcolm, and I had not been contacted by Amanda or anyone else regarding the status of the good faith investigation she said would be conducted. At this point, I was rapidly losing hope, and worried that my complaint had been swept under the rug again.

As each day passed, my hope continued to dwindle, and I found it harder to concentrate in my classes and keep up with my homework. Then something wonderful happened that served as a temporary and much-needed distraction. I was awarded the Performance Excellence Award by Corporate, despite Malcolm's best efforts to sabotage me, for successfully turning around my department and collecting all past due federal funds. I was beaming with pride when Corporate sent the email announcing that I was the recipient of their prestigious award to all Chancellors and student finance staff in the Daebrun division, and when Marisol and Michael received the email, they both ran into my office excitedly.

"Congratulations, boss!" Marisol exclaimed, batting her long eyelashes. "You make me so proud!"

"Me too, Ms. Ebony!" Michael exclaimed. "You're the best boss on the planet!"

Marisol and Michael weren't the only ones at Daebrun who were excited about my accomplishment, a lot of other people were, too. I received congratulatory calls or emails from just about everyone in the Daebrun division, except Malcolm Webb and, surprisingly, Kyle Charron.

One week later, Amanda Ross, the National Director of Human Resources, traveled to the Temple campus to review the results of the good faith investigation, into my discrimination complaint against Malcolm, with me and Dr. Romano.

"Thank you for your patience while we conducted our investigation," Amanda said, twirling the diamond ring on her finger. "After careful review, we determined that Malcolm's actions in canceling your loans were justified because the lender deposited your funds into the Austin bank account in error."

Amanda further explained that by canceling my loans, Malcolm prevented the Austin bank account from being out of balance.

"Our internal investigation has concluded, and the complaint is now closed," she said. "Does this make sense?"

"No, it most certainly does *not* make sense!" I exclaimed. "Because my loan funds were *never* deposited into the Austin bank account!"

"I know this isn't the outcome you were expecting but--"

"Look," I said exasperatedly, interrupting her." My funds were deposited into the Temple account, not the Austin account, and I have a copy of the roster the lender sent with the deposit that proves this fact."

I continued explaining that the deposit roster showed that student loans for me, *and six other students*, were deposited in a lump sum amount into the Temple bank account. If Malcolm truly believed the funds were deposited into the wrong bank account, he would've cancelled the entire deposit, including the loan funds for the other six students. But he didn't do that, he singled me out and canceled my funds only, to delay the stipend check I was expecting, and create a financial hardship for me, just like he created for my sister.

"It would've been nice to have this info during the investigation," Amanda replied, flippantly.

"You would've had it if you conducted a thorough investigation," I immediately responded.

"I really don't appreciate your tone, Ebony," she said, staring at me like I had just insulted the quality of her diamonds. "Like I said, the case is closed, and our decision is final."

After Amanda left, Dr. Romano put her hand on my shoulder.

30

"I'm sorry this happened to you," she said, with compassionate eyes. "For years, people harassed me and my wife, but over time, we let it go because we realized we are not the ones with the problem, they are. Take my advice and let this go."

Are you insane? I thought to myself, as my eyes filled with tears. *Malcolm made my life a living Hell in Austin, and now he's doing the same thing to me in Temple!*

At this point, I was willing to say just about anything to get Dr. Romano to leave. I knew she meant well, but I was tired of talking, and just wanted to be alone.

"You're right, Dr. R. I'll let it go." I said, trying to sound convincing.

After Dr. Romano left and, thankfully, closed the door, I sank deep into my chair, buried my face into both hands, and cried. Then, I sent an email to the Registrar withdrawing from my classes, grabbed my purse and keys, and quickly headed for the door.

When I was safely inside my car, I exploded, "I can't go through this again, Lord, I just can't!"

Then, I sped out of the parking lot completely distraught, and began my commute back to mom's apartment in Austin.

As I was driving, one question consumed my every thought. *If racial discrimination in the workplace is illegal, how was Daebrun able to repeatedly turn a blind eye to Malcolm's racism?*

This question haunted me for miles but as I got closer to home, the answer became crystal clear. Daebrun was able to turn a blind eye because both discrimination complaints I had filed, the anonymous one and this one, were done verbally. And since there was no electronic or paper trail to follow, it would be impossible for me to prove that I had filed a discrimination complaint, or even prove that I notified someone at Daebrun about the discrimination.

I decided then and there that I was going to file a third discrimination complaint, but this time it would be one that Daebrun could not ignore. This time, I would submit a written complaint via email, not anonymously nor verbally, because as far as I was concerned, the 'e' in e-mail stood for evidence. If I was going to start protecting myself from Malcolm, I needed to collect tangible evidence.

When I got home, I sent my first written discrimination complaint, via email, to Amanda Ross, and copied Dr. Romano and Kyle Charron.

From: Ardoin, Ebony
Sent: Tuesday, October 06, 2015 7:26 PM
To: Ross, Amanda
Cc: Romano, Sofie; Charron, Kyle
Subject: Racial Discrimination Complaint Against Malcolm Webb

Dear Ms. Ross,

On September 19, 2015, at 4:13p.m., I called you and filed a verbal discrimination complaint against Malcolm Webb, the Associate Director of Student Finance at the Austin campus. The complaint was based on the phone conversation I had that day with Miguel Vigil, the National Director of Accounting at the Austin campus, in which he informed me that Malcolm had canceled my student loan funds that were deposited into the Temple campus bank account that day, and refunded them to the lender causing a delay in the stipend check I was expecting to receive. At that time, you indicated that you would conduct a good faith investigation and notify me with the results once the investigation was complete.

Today, you informed me that the investigation had concluded, and it was determined that Malcolm's actions in canceling my student loans were justified because, according to you, my loans were deposited into the Austin bank account by the lender in error, and had to be canceled to correct the issue. You also stated that the case was closed, and the decision was final.

This email represents my formal request to reopen the investigation of my discrimination complaint because, as evidenced by the attached deposit roster sent by the lender at the time the deposit was made, my loans were never deposited into the Austin bank account, as you indicated.

Furthermore, the deposit roster shows that my loans, along with the loans for <u>six other students</u>, were deposited in a lump sum amount that day. If Malcolm genuinely thought my loan funds were deposited into the Austin bank account in error, he would've thought the same thing for the other six students and cancelled the entire deposit. But he didn't do that. He singled me out and canceled my loans as another discriminatory act, in a long, sad history of discriminatory acts, to delay my stipend check, and create a financial hardship for me, just like he created for my sister, several months ago.

Earlier this year, I submitted an anonymous discrimination complaint against Malcolm, via the confidential reporting hotline, stating that Black employees in his department were being discriminated against. Daebrun turned a blind eye to that complaint, and has turned a blind eye to the second complaint I verbally filed, as well.

The racial discrimination, racially hostile work environment, racially based preferential treatment of non-Black employees, retaliation, and Daebrun's failure to properly address the issues detailed in both discrimination complaints I made against Malcolm in accordance with Texas state law, as well as its own anti-discrimination policy, has caused me severe and extreme anguish, physical and emotional exhaustion, anxiety, depression, humiliation, anger, nervousness, sleeplessness, embarrassment, fear, and severe emotional distress.

This email represents my third discrimination complaint against Malcolm, and since it's obvious that my well-being doesn't matter to you, my next step is to file a discrimination complaint with the State of Texas Department of Fair Housing and Employment as an employee, and the U.S. Department of Education as a student, because both organizations strictly prohibit racial discrimination, and you, and Daebrun, are in clear violation of state and federal policies.

Thank you for listening. I look forward to hearing from you.

Ebony

I knew that sending an email of this nature was a bold move. But it had to be done, and I was willing to lose my job if it came to it, because I had reached my breaking point.

The next day, I received a frantic phone call from Malcolm.

"Why are you doing this to me?" He screamed. "I made an honest mistake! How can I be a racist? I have Black friends and I'm the least racist person they know!"

Before I could respond, he slammed the phone down in my face.

I never received a response to my email, but two days later, I received a phone call from Latoya, my ex-coworker in Austin, who hadn't said two words to me since the day the anonymous discrimination complaint blew up in our faces.

"Hey girl, just wanted to apologize for being mad," Latoya said.

"That's ok, I'm glad you--"

"I mean, you *did* give me a good reason to be mad at you! I *told* your ass I didn't want nothin' to do with it, but no! You *had* to force the issue and--"

"You call this an apology, Toy?" I said, interrupting her.

"Sorry," she said, with a giggle. "I really called to make sure you heard the news."

"What news?"

"Girl, Malcolm was fired today! Ms. Kelly just announced it!"

"Wow! Seriously? That's the best news I've heard all day!"

After thanking her for her call and hanging up, I sat at my desk in a state of shock replaying her words over and over again in my head.

Then, a tear slowly fell from my eye as her words sunk in, and a wave of relief washed over me. Malcolm's reign of terror came to an end in October 2015, and the email I sent was the catalyst that gave me my first taste of victory fighting racism in the workplace.

One month went by, and for the first time in a long time, things were going well for me personally. My son was living back with me, I moved out of mom's apartment into a nice house that I was renting, and I finally had enough money to pay my bills, and even a few of mom's smaller bills.

Not only were things going well for me personally, but things were also going well for me professionally. My career was going in the right direction again, I had a great boss who supported me, and I received another award, the Chancellor's Award for Employee Excellence, recognizing my efforts in going above and beyond the call of duty at the Temple campus.

The next day, I received another call from Latoya.

"Girl, guess who got promoted to Associate DSF?" She asked.

"Who?"

"The paperboy down the street. Me, dummy!" She said, laughing at her own joke. "And everyone, I mean *everyone*, in the department is walkin' around with chips as big as your head on their shoulders."

Latoya had the least amount of seniority in the Student Finance department in Austin, *and* the least amount of experience. So, I can only imagine how the other team members, especially the manager who trained me, and was demoted, reacted when the announcement was made that she had been promoted to Associate Director of Student Finance.

"Congratulations, Toy! That's great news!"

"Well. Great and not so great."

"What's that supposed to mean?"

Latoya said that when she was promoted, Ms. Kelly increased her salary to thirty-five thousand dollars a year. When I heard this, sirens of every kind sounded loudly in my head. The student finance staff in Austin, as well as the student population, was triple the size of mine in Temple, and her salary as the Associate Director, was less than the salary I made as the Senior Secretary four years ago!

Latoya said she knew she was being underpaid because she overheard Malcolm say that his salary was fifty-five thousand dollars when he was talking to someone on the phone. But when she expressed her concerns about the low salary to Ms. Kelly, she was told that her salary was commensurate with her experience.

After hanging up with Latoya, I thought about my own salary and decided I needed to make getting my degree a priority if I wanted to increase my value as a leader. So, I reenrolled as a student at the Temple campus and registered for classes that began the following week. I was confident I could successfully pass my classes this time now that Malcolm was gone.

Two weeks went by, and things in my classes were going very well. But just when I thought I was out of the woods, Dr. Romano called me to her office. When I arrived, and discovered that Amanda Ross, the wealthy National Director of Human Resources, was on speaker phone, an unsettling feeling came over me.

"Corporate received three anonymous complaints from employees in Temple," Amanda said. "Each one accused you of reverse discrimination against Caucasian employees."

"Come on, this is ridiculous!" I said, frustratingly. "One month after Malcolm's fired, three employees suddenly come forward and file anonymous complaints accusing me of doing the same thing that he was fired for doing?"

To my surprise, Amanda agreed with me. "It's definitely suspicious and doesn't pass the smell test. I've already shared my suspicions with Corporate."

She also said that since no specific information or examples were provided in any of the complaints, there wasn't anything she could investigate. So, the case was closed almost as quickly as it was opened, and no adverse action was taken against me.

Although Malcolm's attempt to frame me was thwarted, I was still very upset. He was finding new ways to retaliate against me, *even after being fired*, ways that had the potential to put my reputation and job at risk.

No longer able to control my emotions, I burst into tears after hanging up with Amanda, as Dr. Romano watched the leader, she once described as made of true grit, crumble before her eyes. Then, she walked over to me, sat down, and took my hand.

35

"I know you're hurting," she said, looking deep into my eyes. "Take comfort in knowing that I'm here for you, and this too shall pass."

After thanking Dr. Romano for her support and encouragement, I returned to my office, closed my door, and silently prayed thanking God, once again, for getting me through yet another ordeal with my reputation and job still intact.

But as I sat at my desk trying to focus on work, I became lightheaded and was overcome with fear. Minutes later, my whole body was shaking like a leaf, I was crying uncontrollably, and was having trouble catching my breath as my heart raced inside my chest.

Oh God, please don't let me die! I thought to myself, unable to verbalize my thoughts. *My son needs me, don't let me die.*

For ten long minutes, I was frozen in fear, and felt like a buffalo was sitting on my chest. Finally, I began to calm down, and was able to take a deep breath. But I was in no condition to go to class, so I immediately left work and began my commute home.

"How am I ever going to earn a degree if I can't even make it to class?" I said, out loud, as I mentally kicked myself for missing class.

As I continued driving, I thought about calling Mom and telling her about the fake accusations Malcolm made against me, and the terrifying experience I had in my office. But after a couple of minutes, I decided against it. I loved her too much to make her worry, and also knew she would insist I go directly to the emergency room, and I didn't want to go.

When I got home, I dragged myself into the house, mustered just enough energy to make my son dinner, then climbed straight into bed, certain I would be sound asleep in a matter of minutes. But as I laid in bed trying to relax, an intense feeling of dread came over me. I started to feel clammy and could barely catch my breath. Terrified, I did the only thing I could think of doing, I called Gabrielle. Gabrielle, my older sister, was mom's mini me, and had a magnetic personality that was equally as beautiful as she was. She was tall like Mom with an hourglass figure, sun kissed skin, long, jet black hair, and mint green eyes. She wore form fitting dresses with high heels, had a walk that could literally stop traffic, and had every man, woman, and child within a fifty-yard radius looking at her.

Gabrielle and I were very close, and I always knew I could count on her to drop everything she was doing, and come to my aid. In fact, one time, I was having a severe migraine and called her. Ten minutes later, she was at my house force feeding me aspirin with one hand, and rubbing the heck out of my forehead with the other. And by the time she was done doing all that rubbing, she had rubbed a layer of skin clean off, and my forehead hurt worse than it did before she rubbed it.

After answering what seemed like a hundred questions, Gabrielle was convinced she knew what was wrong with me.

"Your stressful job is affecting ya health, sis," she said.

"What should I do?"

"You need to find a healthy way to deal with ya stress at work or find another job. It's one or the other."

Then, she showed me a few deep breathing exercises her therapist taught her, gave me a big hug and kiss on the cheek, and then left.

After climbing back into bed, I practiced the deep breathing exercises Gabrielle showed me which, thankfully, helped me relax. And as I started drifting into sweet slumber, I was positive I could control my stress from work, going forward. Afterall, Malcolm had already thrown everything but the kitchen sink at me, and there was nothing left for him to throw...or so I thought.

CHAPTER 5

The Kitchen Sink

In December 2015, Dr. Romano called me to her office to meet with her, as well as Kyle Charron, the National Director of Student Finance, *and* Aaron Burns, the Chief Student Finance Officer at Corporate, who were both on speaker phone. Aaron, the most powerful person in my student finance world, was a heavyset man in his mid-fifties with balding gray hair, a neatly groomed beard, and skin the warmest shade of vanilla. He had iceberg blue eyes, wore power suits of every dark color, and was known in many circles for his directness and uncanny ability to smell talent, as well as bull crap, from a mile away.

Initially, I was relieved when I discovered that no one from Human Resources was on the call, but when I saw the somber look on Dr. Romano's face, I knew, beyond a shadow of a doubt, that Malcolm had found a way to throw the kitchen sink at me.

"I received a letter from the Department of Ed, young lady," Kyle said, with his usual twang. "It seems you're being investigated for ethics violations reported by three students."

Oh no, not again, I thought to myself, as a lumped formed in my throat.

Then, he instructed Dr. Romano to hand me a copy of the letter he received. I was trembling as I read the allegations accusing me of discriminating against White students, giving preferential treatment to Black students, and forging student signatures on federal documents. Before I knew it, tears were streaming down my face.

"We have thirty days to respond," Kyle said. "I reckon we should put Ebony on unpaid leave while we investigate and mull this over."

"I haven't done anything wrong," I cried out in between sniffles, "and I can't afford to go thirty days without a paycheck."

"Wait a minute," Dr. Romano said, jumping into the conversation. "We never discussed putting Ebony on unpaid leave and I'm not okay with this. She's done a terrific job for this campus and is innocent until proven guilty."

Then, thankfully, Aaron chimed into the conversation with a deep voice, and asked me if I recognized the names listed in the complaint.

"No, sir," I tearfully replied. "I don't recognize any of these names."

After receiving my response to his question, Aaron then asked Kyle a direct question.

"Kyle," Aaron said. "When you received the letter, did you check them in our database to verify the legitimacy of the complaints?"

"No, sir," Kyle replied. "I'll do that during the investigation."

Aaron then said he would be right back and put us on hold. As the hold music played, no one said a word, and the tension in the air was so thick you could cut it with a knife.

A few minutes later, Aaron returned to the call.

"Ebony, you can relax," Aaron said. "There are no students at your campus with these names. Do you have any idea what's going on here?"

Before I could respond, Dr. Romano chimed in, and informed Aaron that I was targeted for months by Malcolm Webb, the Associate Director of Student Finance at the Austin campus, who was fired two months ago for racial discrimination. She said she believed Malcolm blamed me for his termination, and made these false allegations, and three others previously, in retaliation.

Aaron agreed with Dr. Romano's assessment and informed Kyle that he would submit the response to the U.S. Department of Education himself to absolve me of any wrongdoing. He also assured me that I had nothing to worry about, my job was not in jeopardy, and the false allegations made against me would not be a dark spot on the bright future I had at Daebrun.

When I made it back to my office, I was full of anxiety. So, I practiced my deep breathing exercises and thanked God for bringing me out of discrimination darkness, once again, with my reputation and job still intact.

As I started working, Michael and Marisol stopped by my office unexpectedly and made my day.

"Happy Birthday!" They yelled in unison.

"Ahh, thanks guys," I said, with the biggest smile on my face.

Then Marisol handed me the balloons she was carrying, and Michael put a chocolate cake on top of my desk.

"You're the best boss a sexy bloke like me could ask for, Ms. Ebony," Michael said, with a laugh.

"Ick," Marisol said, pretending to gag.

And for the next twenty minutes, we had a great time in my office, and I felt so blessed to have such wonderful, caring, and thoughtful employees.

In February 2016, Corporate announced that a federal audit was going to be conducted in the Student Finance department at all Daebrun campuses beginning the following week. The federal audit, conducted by certified public accountants, was a mandatory annual audit all schools who received federal funding were required to pass, by the U.S. Department of Education, to maintain their eligibility to participate in the federal financial aid program.

The federal audit covered fiscal year 2015, which ran from January 1st to December 31st of that year. Since I didn't become the new Director of Student Finance until the latter half of 2015, the audit would test the old processes that were in place before I assumed responsibility.

The day before the audit was scheduled to begin, the lead auditor sent an email to Kyle Charron, the National Director of Student Finance, containing the sample list of student files they were going to audit. When Kyle received the email, he forwarded it to me and Dr. Romano, along with instructions to pull all student files, and have them available for the auditors to review the next day.

When Dr. Romano received Kyle's email, she sent an email to me, and copied Kyle, instructing me to review each student's file and fix all errors before the auditors arrived. So, I spent all day, and most of the night, reviewing each file, fixing all errors (of which there were many), and refunding all federal grant and student loan overpayments. For each refund that was made, the transaction automatically posted to each student's ledger with a date and time stamp. And afterwards, I responded to Dr. Romano's email, and copied Kyle, letting her know that I was finished fixing the errors, and the files were ready for the auditors.

The team of auditors arrived at the Temple campus early the next morning, setup camp in the conference room, and began auditing everything in my department from A to Z. One auditor reviewed student finance policies, standard operating procedures, and cash management records, while the other auditor reviewed student files and ledger transactions.

Because this was my first time participating in an audit of any kind, I didn't know what to expect, and assumed things were going relatively well. That is, until I received a frantic phone call from Kyle.

"What in the Sam Hill did you do after we got the sample, young lady?" He screamed.

"I uh--"

"Are you plum loco? Why in tarnation did you correct the ledgers! The auditors failed your campus and now they're leaving! Do you know how serious this is? We could lose our federal funding because of you, and you could lose your job!"

As Kyle continued screaming at me, I was trembling and beside myself with worry because he said I could lose my job. And I was so confused. Dr. Romano copied Kyle on the email she sent instructing me to fix everything before the auditors arrived. If he knew I wasn't supposed to do that, why didn't he say something when it could've made a difference?

"You were copied on the email Dr. Romano sent telling me to fix the errors," I said, trying to explain. "Why didn't you tell me not to correct-- "

"Oh no you don't!" Kyle said, forcefully interrupting me. *"You're not sticking' my foot in this steaming pile of meadow muffins!"*

I sat quietly with the phone held to my ear, as tears began to fall. I didn't know what to do or say to make things better, and I was worried beyond belief. Then, Kyle cleared his throat and said, "What I'm trying to say is, first you blame Malcolm for your failures, and now you're trying to blame me for your mistakes. Didn't nobody never teach you to own your actions?"

Although I couldn't see him, I suspected that Kyle was enjoying the situation I had unknowingly found myself in, and wondered if setting me up to fail was his intention all along.

"I- I'm going to talk to Dr. Romano to see if we can fix this," I said, wiping away my tears with my hand. "I'll call you back."

After hanging up, I ran as fast as I could in my two-inch heels to Dr. Romano's office, and when I told her what happened, she was just as alarmed as I was.

"Oh my God," she quietly said, through teary eyes. "Ebony, it's not your job that's in danger, it's mine. I will be fired because of this and we just bought a house."

"Isn't there anything we can do, Dr. R?" I asked.

"It doesn't hurt to try."

A few minutes later, we sprinted to the conference room where the auditors were packing up to leave and requested to speak with the lead auditor. Then, Dr. Romano fell on her sword, and through tears of her own explained that she had mistakenly instructed me to make corrections after the sample list was received. She also said that because I was new to management and had no previous audit experience, I had no way of knowing that the instructions she gave me were wrong.

The lead auditor was touched by Dr. Romano's willingness to own her mistake, and agreed to proceed with the audit, but under the condition that a finding would be issued for every ledger with a time stamp that showed a correction was made after the sample list was emailed to Kyle. Dr. Romano agreed to the terms because anything was better than an automatic fail.

Although I was grateful to the auditor for proceeding with the audit, the remainder of the week was nerve-wracking because I was well aware of the number of ledger corrections I had made that would be cited as findings. This made it impossible for me to focus on my classes, so I missed the entire week and couldn't catch up on missing assignments. To make matters worse, I failed my classes, and was no longer eligible to receive tuition reimbursement which hurt me financially.

When the audit was finished at the end of the week, the lead auditor conducted an exit meeting with me and Dr. Romano, who were sitting in the conference room, and Kyle Charron and Aaron Burns, the Chief Student Finance Officer at Corporate, who were both on speaker phone.

When she announced that my department received nine whopping audit findings, the most she'd ever issued to one campus in her entire career, I wanted to crawl under a rock to hide my shame.

"Under normal circumstances, your department would've failed this audit," she said, looking directly at me. "But I'm going to conditionally pass you this time, since you were not the leader during the audit period. But if next year's audit results are equally as horrendous, you will fail the audit and lose eligibility to participate in the federal financial aid program."

Although the results were "horrendous", Dr. Romano and I were relieved that she issued a conditional pass for our campus this time, and neither one of us lost our jobs.

The next morning, Aaron Burns scheduled a conference call to review the audit results with me and Dr. Romano, who were in Dr. Romano's office, and Kyle Charron, who was on speaker phone.

"The audit results for your campus are mortifying," Aaron said, in a direct way, with no attempt to sugar coat it. "Temple received nine audit findings which is not only embarrassing, but also puts your campus at risk of losing financial aid eligibility."

"I'm sorry," I said, trying to stop my voice from quivering. "I'll do better next year."

"You weren't the leader during the audit period," Aaron replied. "You are not responsible."

"I agree with Aaron," Dr. Romano said, jumping into the conversation. "You've done an awesome job and have made tremendous strides in turning things around."

I fully expected Kyle to chime in and offer some words of encouragement, too, but all you could hear from his end of the phone was silence. He was the only person on the call who didn't say a single word which, I think, is partially the reason Aaron's focus shifted from me to him.

"Kyle, if I'm not mistaken, you *were* the National Director the entire 2015 year," he said. "Help me understand the reason the issues at the Temple campus were not on your radar."

"They *were* on my radar," Kyle replied, sounding defensive. "That's why I been trying to centralize."

Centralizing meant that a third-party organization assumed responsibility for completing most of the work done by the student finance staff at all Daebrun campuses. If centralizing was approved, the student finance departments at all campuses would be downsized, more than half of the student finance staff would lose their jobs, and the responsibility for passing future federal audits would fall squarely on the shoulders of the third-party organization, not Kyle.

Aaron ignored Kyle's comments about centralizing and turned his focus back on me.

"So we don't get caught with our pants down again next year, Ebony," he said, "I'm going to send my Corporate Director of SF to your campus in a couple of weeks, to assess operations and audit your current files and processes. We cannot afford to have another disastrous audit."

Two weeks later, Steve Burger, the Corporate Director of Student Finance, arrived at the Temple campus. He was a tall drink of water in his early forties with an athletic build, pale skin, wavy hair as dark as black blossoms, and intense, golden eyes. He wore a charcoal gray suit with black stylish shoes, and when I saw him standing in a power stance at the reception desk, I instantly knew that one bad word from Steve would have me effectively relocated to the unemployment line.

The first hour of our time together was tense as I demonstrated the streamlined, technology-based processes I developed as he observed with a concerned look on his face. But as each hour passed, the concern he had disappeared and was replaced by fascination, and I was tickled when he insisted on switching chairs with me so he could operate my computer himself to test my processes.

On our last day together, he reviewed a multitude of student files while I observed and did his absolute best to find something wrong with at least one of them. For hours on end, he reviewed file after file and could not find a single thing wrong with any of them. By the end of his visit, he was so excited about the condition of my department and had no doubts we would pass the next audit with flying colors.

The next day, he emailed his report to Aaron Burns and copied me, Dr. Romano, and Kyle Charron.

From: Burger, Steve
Sent: Friday, March 11, 2016 3:44 PM
To: Burns, Aaron
Cc: Ardoin, Ebony; Romano, Sofie; Charron, Kyle

I was over the moon with excitement when I read the results of Steve's operational assessment, and couldn't wait to share the news with mom, and my son.

Although the last four years of my employment were filled with ordeal after painful ordeal of both blatant and veiled racial discrimination, I was filled with optimism, and truly believed that with Steve Burger on my side, I would finally have an equal opportunity to succeed based on my performance and character...or so I thought.

CHAPTER 6

Another Day, Another Racist

One week after Steve Burger, the Corporate Director of Student Finance, left the Temple campus, I received a surprising phone call that put my career on the fast track.

"Hello, Ebony," a male voice on the other end of the phone said. "This is Aaron Burns, the Chief Student Finance Officer at Corporate."

Oh man, what's going on now? I thought to myself, as my heart fell into my stomach.

I didn't have anything against Aaron, but every time I was on a call with him, it was because something bad had happened. He was on the call when I found out that Malcolm retaliated against me after he was fired, and he was also the one who described the audit results for my department as mortifying on the post-audit conference call.

"Hi Aaron," I replied, with a little hesitation. "How can I help you?"

To my surprise, he wasn't calling to be the bearer of more bad news. He was calling to congratulate me on the outstanding report he received from Steve Burger, after he assessed operations in my department.

"I want to review the processes that knocked the socks off Steve," Aaron said, in his usual direct way. "Steve is tough, and it's not easy to impress him, but he was impressed by you."

If I could've done a cartwheel without breaking a few bones I would have! I couldn't believe it! My hard work and efforts got the attention of the most powerful person in my student finance world, and not in a bad way either.

After we hung up, I immediately emailed my process documentation, including flowcharts, standard operating procedures, and training materials, to Aaron, per his request. About three hours later, he called again.

"Your processes are fantastic!" He exclaimed.

"Thank you, that really means a lot coming from you," I replied.

"I want you to demonstrate your processes on the next SF Leadership Call," Aaron continued. "And train the other directors on implementation."

The SF Leadership Call was a weekly conference call that all senior directors, directors, and associate directors of student finance at over seventy campuses owned by Corporate were required to attend. The call was mandatory because it was the primary way Corporate provided training, and communicated important information related to student finance operations.

"It would be my pleasure!" I exclaimed, excitedly. "Thank you for this opportunity!"

After I hung up, I grabbed my keys and purse, and left work for the day. As I was driving home, I received a call from mom.

"Hey, whatcha doing?"

"Smiling! I had a spectacular day, mom!"

"Oh? Well, don't keep me in suspense."

Then I shared the great news with Mom who was equally as excited as I was.

"I'm so proud of ya, honey! God is good!"

The following week, I invited Michael and Marisol to join me in my office as I made my debut as a trainer on the SF Leadership Conference Call. For almost two hours, I trained over seventy student finance leaders and their staff on how to implement the processes I developed. The training went extremely well, and afterwards, I received a multitude of calls and emails from other student finance directors requesting my assistance with implementing my processes at their campuses. I even received an email from the Corporate Director of Training.

From: Mikelson, Roger

Sent: Thursday, March 24, 2016 2:41 PM

To: Ardoin, Ebony

Cc: Burns, Aaron; Burger, Steve; Romano, Sofie

Subject: Your Processes

Ebony,

> *I, and many others, were very impressed with the training presentation you gave today. I would like to use your presentation, with a few adjustments, to develop a corporate training that I plan to roll out to all campuses in the near future. Please call me to discuss the excellent model you provided and to share your expertise as soon as possible.*
>
> *Thanks,*
>
> *Roger Mikelson, Corporate Director of Training*

I was delighted by the success of the first large scale training I'd ever given, and thanked God for blessing me with the opportunity to share my skills with so many people in the student finance world.

Now, you're probably thinking that everything from this point forward was smooth sailing, and the racial discrimination I had previously endured was a thing of the past, right? Wrong.

The next morning, Kyle Charron, the National Director of Student Finance, traveled to the Temple campus under a shadow of secrecy, and walked into my office unannounced. I didn't have any meetings scheduled with him and had no idea he was planning to visit. So, when I saw him, it caught me off guard and before I knew it, he was standing in front of my desk, and dumping on me like I was his very own personal toilet.

"Wanna know what I realized yesterday, young lady?" He asked furiously, with nostrils flaring as he sat down. "I realized you're another snake in the grass trying to bite me."

I didn't want my staff to hear, so I got up, walked over, and closed the door. Then, I calmly returned to my desk and sat back down.

"I'm sorry but I have no idea what you're talking about," I replied.

"*You knew* I was trying to centralize," he continued, "and this little stunt you pulled made me look bad and ruined my chances."

"What stunt?" I asked, confused.

Kyle leaned back in his chair and crossed his legs. "You think you're slick, don't ya? A slick, slippery snake in the grass."

I didn't say a word.

"You know what happens to snakes in the grass where I'm from?" He asked, narrowing his eyes at me as the veins in his temple throbbed.

I remained silent, refusing to dignify his question with a response.

"When we see a snake in the grass," Kyle continued, putting emphasis on each word, "we get a shovel and chop its head off."

Again, I didn't respond.

"You don't see me as your superior, do you? You don't call me with questions or askin' for my help anymore. So, who are you calling 'cause it damn sure ain't me."

Unable to contain my anger any longer, I blurted out and said, "The first time I called you for help you said, and I quote, 'if you can't do this job, we'll find someone who can', and the last time we spoke, you accused me of blaming Malcolm for my failures and you for my mistakes. You've never provided any kind of training or guidance to help me, so why on earth would I call you for anything?"

"You're full of so much shit your skin is brown!" He yelled, spraying spit across my desk.

I was stunned. First Ms. Kelly, then Malcolm Webb, and now Kyle Charron? Were racists standing in some invisible line waiting for their chance to take me down? And if so, how long was the line?

At this point, I no longer felt comfortable being alone with Kyle, so I paged Dr. Romano over the intercom system.

"Was that really necessary?" he asked, trying to hide his anger with a fake smile.

Ignoring Kyle, I sat quietly waiting for Dr. Romano to respond to my page. A couple of minutes later, she called, and Kyle listened as I explained everything that had happened, including the threat about chopping my head off and the racist comment he made. After hanging up, the room was so quiet you could hear a pin drop, and there was palpable tension in the air.

When Dr. Romano arrived at my office, she came in, closed the door, and sat down in the chair next to Kyle.

"Showing up in Ebony's office unannounced making accusations, threats, and racist comments is highly inappropriate."

"She didn't follow the chain of command!" Kyle yelled. "She went over my head and made me look bad!"

Dr. Romano told Kyle that I was specifically asked by Corporate to share processes that were working well at our campus, and that I wasn't trying to hurt him. She also said that he owed me an apology.

Kyle never apologized, but instead changed the subject stating that he was going on vacation, and would reach out to me to sort things out when he returned.

After he left, Dr. Romano took me to lunch to further discuss what happened and calm my nerves because I was still shaken up by the whole experience.

"If I had a dollar for every racist--"

"That's funny," Dr. Romano said, interrupting me as she laughed.

"How about this one? Another day, another racist." I said, trying to keep my eyes from tearing up.

"That's funny, too," Dr. Romano sadly said. "Do you want to file a complaint with HR?" She asked.

"No, I've already filed three discrimination complaints," I responded. "I don't want to add to the rumors labeling me as the girl who cried racism."

When I got back to work, Michael came to see me.

"Ms. Ebony, I heard that jerk yelling at you in your office."

"I'm sorry you had to hear that."

"It's okay, Ms. Ebony. He's lucky Dr. R came in before I did. I was gonna bust in and show him my wax on wax off," Michael said, as he pretending to kick the air. "You're the best boss on the planet. I'll always have your back."

Then, Michael walked around my desk, gave me a friendly hug, and then left.

Two weeks later, Kyle returned from vacation, and the next day, an organizational announcement was emailed to all staff and faculty stating that Kyle had resigned from his position as National Director of Student Finance for personal reasons. When I received the email, I asked Dr. Romano if his resignation was a result of the racist meltdown he had in my office before he went on vacation.

"I think his departure had less to do with you, and more to do with the poor audit results, Corporate's lack of confidence in his ability to lead, and perhaps the phone call I made to Aaron Burns about the threat and racist comments he made to you," she said, with a sly smile.

After finding out that Dr. Romano called Aaron Burns to protect me from further discrimination from Kyle, I knew she was someone I could trust and who would always have my back, and I was grateful to finally have another great boss.

My reputation as a process guru continued to grow, and over the next month, I was sought out by student finance leaders at various colleges owned by Corporate requesting to train with me at my campus. I even received a call from Amanda Ross, the former National Director of Human Resources at the Austin campus, who was promoted to Chancellor following what was rumored to be a forced resignation by Ms. Kelly.

"You've developed quite a reputation as the process expert," she said, with a smile that I'm sure was as bright as her diamonds.

"Thanks, Amanda. That means a lot coming from you."

"I'm calling because I need your help. Latoya Lawson was promoted to Associate DSF after Malcolm was terminated, but she's struggling and needs training. Would you be willing to spend a few days here helping her get a better understanding of SF operations as a personal favor to me?"

When Amanda asked me to come to the Austin campus, I thought I was going to be sick. That campus, which I described to Mom as a cesspool of evil, held so many painful memories, and left so many invisible scars that, to this day, had not healed. But it broke my heart to know that my dear friend Latoya was struggling, and I winced when I thought of the training, or lack thereof, that she, undoubtedly, received from Kyle.

"It would be my pleasure to help," I replied.

Two weeks later, I arrived at the Austin campus, and was greeted by Latoya moments after I had checked in with the receptionist.

"Girl, it's good to see you!" She said, with a smile that could sink a ship.

After exchanging pleasantries in the lobby, we began to walk down the hallway, as Latoya talked a million miles a minute. But as we continued walking, my heart began to race and I zoned out, as memories of Ms. Kelly, and the emotional, verbal, and mental abuse she inflicted on me, haunted me like a phantom in the night.

And as we approached the entry way to the Student Finance department, terror struck again, as memories of Malcolm, the evil in his eyes, and the hatred in his soul, moved through me like a landslide, and I was afraid.

51

After taking a few deep breaths, and reminding myself that Ms. Kelly and Malcolm were both gone and no longer able to hurt me, the fear subsided, and all was calm again.

Once we were behind closed doors in Latoya's office, safe from prying eyes and ears, the chit chat was abruptly cut short and she began to vent.

"Girl, remember I told you Ms. Kelly gave me a funky thirty-five thousand when they promoted me, even though Malcolm was getting paid fifty-five G's to do the same job?"

"Yeah, that really stinks."

"Well yesterday, I looked up the salaries for my employees and discovered that almost half of them *make more money than me! That's some bullshit!*"

Latoya continued venting, saying that she informed Amanda Ross of her discovery, and requested a salary increase. And Amanda told her the same thing Ms. Kelly had said--she would be paid more when she gained more experience.

I really wanted to help Latoya gain the experience she needed to get the raise she so richly deserved, so over the next five days, we trained from sunup to sundown on everything she needed to know. And at the end of our time together, Latoya had a detailed understanding of student finance operations, and had hopefully gained the experience she needed to negotiate a higher salary. The next day, I sent an email to Latoya, and copied Amanda Ross, detailing every aspect of training that Latoya received, as proof of the management experience she gained.

As I drove home from the Austin campus, and reflected on the last four years of my employment, the accomplishments I achieved, the racism I survived, the allies I made, and the people I helped, I was proud of how far I'd come in my career with Daebrun, and confident the dark days of racism were finally behind me…or so I thought.

CHAPTER 7

She Hates Me, She Hates Me Not

Things at work were great for the next five months, but in August 2016, fear was put in the heart of every leader from the Chancellor at each campus on down, when Corporate announced the appointment of Dr. Harry Gershon as the Chief Executive Officer (CEO) for the Daebrun division. Dr. Gershon was a beefy man in his sixties with peach hued skin, pinkish cheeks, sea green eyes, and balding gray hair. He was a well-respected politician in the state of Texas, had a tough as nails approach to leadership, and was feared by many in our organization because of his reputation for shaking things up.

During his first month in office, Dr. Gershon stayed true to his reputation, and made an organizational change at the Temple campus that threatened the trajectory of my career. Dr. Romano, the Chancellor and second-best boss I ever had, was fired by Dr. Gershon for unknown reasons, and replaced by Karen Taylor, one of the most conservative people I had ever met. She was a gangly woman in her mid-fifties with pale skin, sunken cheeks, and brown eyes as dark as night. She had toffee brown hair worn in a modest bun, dressed in long skirts with blouses buttoned up to her neck, and wore sensible shoes made for comfort not style.

Dr. Taylor, much like Ms. Kelly, hated me right from the start, and avoided me like I had the plague during her first two weeks in office. She wanted nothing to do with me, so in an effort to limit our contact, she changed my reporting structure so that I no longer reported to her, and instead now reported to Logan MacDougal, the Vice President of Finance. Logan was a man in his late thirties with light green eyes, dark brown hair cut in a French crop, peach colored skin, and more freckles than there were stars in the sky. He had broad shoulders from years of weightlifting, dressed in business casual attire, and was genuinely happy to have me on his team.

As the weeks went by, Dr. Taylor found it increasingly difficult to limit interactions with me, even after changing my reporting structure, because I was the only one on campus who had answers to her questions related to student finance operations. But one day, as we were walking down the hallway together, she said something to me that really rubbed me the wrong way.

"I've never seen hair like yours," she said, casually. "Reminds me of earthworms."

When I heard her off-handed comment, it didn't take a rocket scientist to figure out that she was taking a subtle jab at my dookie braids, the same braids my first and best boss at Daebrun, Dr. Hunter Hall, said reminded him of a Nubian queen.

The off-handed comments from Dr. Taylor didn't stop there. A week later, she made another comment that made me cringe, after I gave my departmental update during our first campus management meeting with her at the helm.

"Wow, Ebony," she said, "You are so articulate. If you weren't sitting right here in front of me, I'd never know you're Black."

What the hell is that supposed to mean? I thought to myself, as everyone nodded in agreement.

At this point, alarms were going off in my head, along with a neon sign flashing *RACIST AHEAD PROCEED WITH CAUTION!*

I really wanted to give Dr. Taylor the benefit of the doubt and not automatically assume that she was yet another racist, but after everything I had endured with Ms. Kelly, Malcolm Webb, and Kyle Charron, I wasn't taking any chances. And since written documentation and tangible evidence worked so well in my fight against Malcolm's racism, I decided to create weapons consisting of both that I could use to protect my career and defend myself if it turned out that my suspicions about Dr. Taylor were correct.

Initially, the thought of secretly recording all future conversations that she would undoubtedly have with me, using my smart phone, crossed my mind, especially since I knew that Texas was a one-party consent state that approved of secretly recording conversations you are a party to, but I worried about getting caught. So instead, I decided to create a document that I could use to keep track of conversations with Dr. Taylor, named it Daily Log, and inserted a three-column table with Date, Time, and Description headers. Then, using my memory, as well as emails I had received and sent, I documented everything of importance in my Daily Log, starting with the day I transferred to the Temple campus, and ending with the racist comment Dr. Taylor made about the way I spoke. Once everything that had occurred in the past was entered, my Daily Log became a living document that I would update daily as new conversations and events involving Dr. Taylor occurred.

Next, I saved copies of all emails and documents related to my employment at Daebrun, using a free online cloud storage website I found on the internet. Not only did I save a copy of the discrimination complaint email against Malcolm that I sent, but I also saved copies of the emails I received from all sources regarding my outstanding performance, and awards I received, as proof that I was performing my job at a very high level before Dr. Taylor was hired. This was important because I remembered when Malcolm retaliated against me for filing the anonymous discrimination complaint, he changed the work I had completed, and riddled it with errors to make it appear I was an incompetent employee, so he could justify firing me. By saving the emails pertaining to my outstanding performance and the awards I won, I had tangible proof that I was not only an outstanding employee, but I was also an employee who was recognized for going above and beyond the call of duty.

Finally, I saved copies of my employment agreement, the employee handbook, a copy of Daebrun's anti-discrimination policy, and my last paycheck stub, because if things got bad, and I needed to retain an attorney, I knew these items might come in handy.

With the weapons I created in my arsenal, I felt a little better about my ability to protect myself from Dr. Taylor, if necessary.

Although I was worried about Dr. Taylor being a racist, things at work were going better than ever! My department consistently led the Daebrun division in packages completed each week, our campus was breaking cash collection records due to my team's excellent packaging rates, and best of all, it seemed as though I had earned the respect and support of Dr. Gershon, the new CEO for the Daebrun division. In an email to Dr. Taylor, he wrote:

> *From: Gershon, Harry*
> *Sent: Monday, October 17, 2016 7:21 AM*
> *To: Taylor, Karen*
> *Subject: Fantastic Packaging Rate*
>
> *Karen,*
> *Congratulations on the 99% packaging rate! Tell Ebony how proud I am of her!*
> *Harry*

It also appeared that I had earned Dr. Taylor's respect and support as well, because she copied me, and my new boss, Logan MacDougal, on her response to Dr. Gershon's email in which she wrote:

> *From: Taylor, Karen*
> *Sent: Tuesday, October 18, 2016 8:02 AM*
> *To: Gershon, Harry*
> *Cc: Ardoin, Ebony; MacDougal, Logan*
> *Subject: RE: Fantastic Packaging Rate*
>
> *Thank you, Harry. I am very proud of Ebony, as well. It won't be long before she reaches 100%!*
>
> *Karen*

When I read Dr. Taylor's response, I was pleasantly surprised. I was also thoroughly confused because I couldn't imagine a scenario where a racist would be proud of a Black person. So, I decided to put my suspicions about Dr. Taylor on the backburner, and give her the benefit of the doubt, once again. I also convinced myself that the racist comments she had previously made were isolated incidents, and decided to stop maintaining the state of hypervigilance I had become accustomed to over the years.

As I was driving home from work, I called Mom to share the good news about how well things were going, and to check on her. I didn't see her as often as I did before I moved out of her apartment, and wanted to make sure she was doing okay.

"Hey, mom. Whatcha doin?"

"Layin' down. Me and Gabby just got back from the doctor."

"Oh no. Are you constipated again?"

"Yeah."

"Did he figure out what's causing it?"

"He said a small mass formed in my intestine, and it's creatin' a blockage. I'm havin' surgery next week to remove the mass."

When Mom said she was scheduled for surgery, I felt like the wind had been knocked out of me. So, I pulled over to the side of the highway.

"Y- You're having surgery, mom?!" I said, as my eyes filled with tears, and my heart raced.

"Don't get yourself worked up, honey," Mom replied. "It's a routine procedure, and the doc said I'll be done in about forty-five minutes."

"Routine procedure? Thank God." I said, breathing a huge sigh of relief. "That doesn't sound too bad at all."

The following week, Gabrielle and I went to the hospital for mom's surgery, and as Mom laid in her hospital bed, we laughed, cracked jokes, and acted silly, exhibiting behaviors that came naturally to us whenever we were together, which helped Mom relax. That is, until we crossed the threshold from being entertaining to annoying.

"Okay, that's enough, you two," Mom said, with a slight smile.

After about thirty minutes, a man came into the room to get mom, but before we let him take her, we held mom's hands, and Gabrielle said a prayer.

"God, you're the doctor that's never lost a patient," Gabby prayed. "We ask you to guide the hands performing mom's surgery, and heal her from the inside out if it is your will. In Jesus holy name we pray, Amen."

Then I kissed Mom on her forehead, and Gabrielle kissed her cheek, and with that, she was wheeled away.

The surgery was supposed to be a routine procedure that only lasted forty-five minutes. But it had been four hours, and we were still sitting in the waiting room. No one told us anything, and every time we asked what was going on, they gave us some bullshit answer.

"I'm scared." I said, trying not to jump to conclusions.

"Me too," Gabrielle responded. "I can't imagine why it's taking so long."

Not only were we afraid something was terribly wrong, but our relatives were afraid, too. Every fifteen minutes, an aunt, uncle, or cousin would call to find out if we had heard anything.

Three more hours passed, and we were still sitting in the waiting room, anxious to see our mom, and worried beyond belief.

Finally, the elevator door opened, and we saw mom's doctor walking towards us. As he got closer to the waiting area we were in, we stood up to greet him, but I could tell by the somber look on his face that something was, in fact, terribly wrong.

"We did everything we could," the doctor sadly said.

"Oh my God!" I muttered, as I lost my balance and fell backwards, almost missing my chair.

At that moment, everything around me disappeared into a gray haze, and I felt dizzy. As I slumped in my chair, all I could see was the doctor standing in front of Gabrielle, speaking in what appeared to be slow motion, as my heart pounded so hard, I thought it would burst through my chest.

"Is Mom alive?" Gabrielle screamed, as tears streamed down her face.

"Yes, she's in recovery, but I'm afraid I have bad news," the doctor continued. "During surgery, we discovered that Babette has colon cancer, and it has spread."

Gabrielle started crying hysterically, as I remained in a state of perpetual shock. I wanted to cover my mouth with both hands to keep from screaming, but my arms felt like two limp noodles as the words *your mother has colon cancer* hit me like a ton of bricks. Before I knew it, I had let out a blood curdling scream, and began begging God at the top of my lungs to save mom.

"What does that mean? It can be treated, right?" Gabrielle nervously asked, as a river of tears rolled down her cheeks. "She's going to be okay, right?"

The doctor explained that the cancer was at stage four, and looked like tiny grains of sand thrown all over mom's other organs.

"But mom's going to be okay, right?" I cried, repeating Gabrielle's question, in case he didn't hear it the first time.

The doctor was silent, and it was so quiet I could hear my heart beating. Then after a few of the longest minutes of my life, he responded.

"I'm sorry, but Babette doesn't have much time. After she's released from the hospital, we'll begin chemotherapy to try to slow things down."

Then, the doctor took us to mom's room where she was recovering, and we surrounded her with love and emotional support, as the doctor gave her the devastating news. Mom was inconsolable.

"I can't have cancer," she said, with a weak and shaky voice as tears streamed down her face. "There's gotta be some mistake. I have a mass. That's it. A mass."

To say this was the most difficult and painful moment of my entire life is a severe understatement. In a matter of minutes, the world I knew came crashing down around me. Mom, the woman who adopted me, loved me, and had been a caregiver to me my whole life, was now the one in need of care. She was diagnosed with colon cancer, one of the deadliest forms of cancer in the world, and it was at stage four, her doctor said, the final stage before Mom would die. I was grief-stricken, and prayed chemotherapy would be enough to hold the cancer at bay, because Mom wasn't just the woman who raised me, she was my very best friend in the world, and losing her to cancer was not an option.

After receiving the horrific news, there was absolutely no way I could leave mom's side to go to work the next day. So, even though it was late, I called my new boss, Logan, on his cell phone, explained what happened, and requested a week off from work to be with mom.

"I'm sorry to hear that, Ebony," Logan said. "Go ahead and take the week off and don't worry about work,"

"Thank you, Logan."

"You know, my weightlifting buddy's dad had colon cancer, but now it's in remission. Miracles do happen, and I pray your Mom has the same results."

"That's encouraging. I really appreciate it."

"No problem. Who do you want to put in charge while you're out?"

"Marisol," I replied. "She has seniority and has the most experience."

As I sat in the chair next to mom's bed, and draped the blanket I received from the nurse over me, I received an unexpected call from Dr. Taylor, the new Chancellor.

"I just spoke with Logan," she said. "I'm sorry to hear about your mother."

"Thank you," I replied. "It really means a lot to me that you called."

"He said you'll be gone for a week, and I instructed him to put Michael in charge. When you return, let's talk about adding a remote workday to your schedule, to give you extra time to be with your mother."

"Will do," I replied. "Thank you for your support."

After we hung up, I felt an undeniable sense of relief. Dr. Taylor was surprisingly supportive and, dare I say, even compassionate. And while I didn't fully understand the reason she wanted Michael to be put in charge instead of Marisol, I wasn't going to look a gift horse in the mouth. I was grateful for the kindness she had shown me, and knew, beyond a shadow of a doubt, that Dr. Taylor didn't hate me like I originally thought she did, and my fears about her being a racist were completely unfounded...or so I thought.

CHAPTER 8

OMG, She's a Racist!

During the week Mom was in the hospital recovering, I was stressed to the max. I visited her every day, and did my best to put on a brave face even though I was an emotional wreck on the inside. And I wasn't the only one having a difficult time dealing with mom's cancer diagnosis. Gabrielle was falling apart at the seams, too. I'll never forget the day we were at the hospital spending time with Mom during an already emotional time, when the doctor who was on duty walked in with a team of residents.

"This patient is a fifty-five-year-old female diagnosed with metastatic colon cancer," he nonchalantly said, looking down at the chart in his hand.

Gabrielle jumped to her feet, and with blazing eyes of fury, lit into him like a torch.

"This patient is our mom, you asshole! How dare you come in here with these people and blurt out she has cancer like you're ordering a fucking pizza!"

The doctor, who was shocked by Gabrielle's strong reaction, widened his eyes as his jaw dropped, and immediately apologized for his lapse in judgment and poor bedside manner. Then, he asked the residents to leave, and proceeded to care for Mom with the dignity and tenderness she deserved.

"Who do you have there, Ms. Babette?" He asked, with the warmest of smiles as he pointed to the big, purple penguin she was holding in her arms.

"Molly the Magic Penguin," Mom replied, with a childlike smile that lit up the room.

Molly the Magic Penguin was a stuffed animal in the collection of stuffed animals Mom had amassed over the years. She won it on her birthday a decade ago, along with fifteen hundred dollars and a souvenir jacket, at a casino with the last five dollars she had. And after collecting her winnings that day, Mom was convinced there was something special about her penguin, and it had a place in her heart ever since.

When I brought Molly to Mom that day, it lifted her spirits and put the first smile on her face I had seen since the day she was diagnosed with cancer. Sadly, the smile didn't last long. The next day when I visited her, I could tell by her puffy, red eyes that she had been crying before I arrived at the hospital. When I walked in, and sat down next to her, she looked at me with the same loving eyes I had seen my entire life, but they were heavy, and full of sadness. Then, Mom took my hand.

"I'm not afraid a dyin', honey--"

"You're not going to die mom," I said, immediately interrupting her. "You're going to be okay."

I didn't mean to stop Mom in mid-sentence, but I couldn't handle the thought of Mom dying let alone talk about it.

"I know ya scared, honey. I'm scared, too," she said, with tear-soaked eyes. "But please. Please let me talk about what's scarin' me."

As Mom looked at me through her beautiful, weary eyes, I closed my eyes for a few seconds, and swallowed hard.

"Okay, mom," I said, with a quivering voice. "I'm listening."

"Thank you, honey," she said, as she held my hand tight, and gave me a small smile. "I'm not afraid a dyin', 'cause I know Jesus is gonna be right there waitin' for me."

Then she started to cry, and as the tears rolled down her face she said, "I just don't wanna leave you kids. Ya not ready to be without me and I know it."

As Mom cried and shared her deepest thoughts with me, I cried, too, and actively listened as Mom talked about her fears, things she would miss, regrets she had, and things she still wanted to do in life. And as painful as the conversation was, I was glad I put mom's need to talk before my need to stay in denial.

That afternoon, Gabrielle and I moved Mom from her small apartment on the east side of town, to a two-bedroom apartment closer to Gabrielle's house on the southwest side of town. Moving Mom was no easy task by any stretch of the imagination, because she was a bit of a hoarder, especially when it came to books. Mom had hundreds of old, dusty books going all the way back to 1960, and every time Gabrielle and I tried to talk her into getting rid of them, she'd refuse, and say she might need them. In fact, one day, I tried to convince Mom to get rid of one old book. Just one. In hopes that she would realize she didn't need it, and a pattern would start.

"Mom, I'm going to throw this book away, okay?" I asked, after grabbing an old 1960's book on learning how to type with a typewriter from the shelf.

Mom's radar immediately went up. Then, she said, "Lemme take a look at it."

And after examining it from every angle, and flipping it over a few times, she said, "No, put it back. I was just sayin' to my friend Dottie the other day that I need to find my book and learn how to type."

Five hours and a glass of wine later, we got everything moved to the new apartment.

None of the furniture in mom's bedroom matched. So, to surprise her, I bought her a gently used bedroom suite, including a smaller queen size bed, to make room for the clunky oxygen concentrator, and Gabrielle bought her new bedding with matching curtains to go with the new furniture. And when Mom got to her new apartment, saw that everything was put away and in order, and saw the new bedroom furniture, her spirit was lifted, and she was happy to be home.

The next day, I returned to work after being off for a week to be with Mom and scheduled a meeting with Marisol and Michael to catch up, and review our goals for the week. It was then that I started having problems with Michael.

"Welcome back, boss!" Marisol exclaimed. "We missed you!"

"I didn't," Michael replied under his breath, avoiding eye contact with me.

"Thank you, Marisol. It's good to be back," I replied. "Michael, did you say something?"

He didn't say a word. He just rolled his eyes. So, I continued.

"Marisol, did you have any issues while I was away?" I asked.

"The only thing that I wanted to ask was--"

"Why are you asking her? I was in charge!" Michael rudely said, interrupting Marisol. "And no, we didn't have any issues!"

"Pendejo!" Marisol replied, flicking her hair back and chiming in. "Your being very rude, Michael."

Michael continued being belligerent and overly aggressive, so I asked Marisol to leave because she was clearly getting upset. When she left and closed the door behind her, I confronted Michael.

"The way you are behaving is concerning," I said. "What's going on?"

"I don't have time for this!" He exclaimed.

And with that, he got up, and stormed out of my office.

I was speechless. Normally, Michael was a model employee, even though he was arrogant and full of himself, who worked hard, and respected me. But while I was gone, his arrogance was taken to a whole new level, and it seemed like he had morphed into a completely different person while I was gone.

I didn't want to cause a scene or report him to Human Resources on my first day back, so instead, I called my boss, Logan, for guidance.

"I'm on my way to the gym to pump some iron," Logan said. "What's up?"

"No worries. I was just wondering if something happened while I was away. I just had a team meeting, and Michael was in rare form."

"Really? How so?"

"He was acting *way* out of character. Questioning my decisions, challenging my authority, rolling his eyes as I spoke, and behaving aggressively. And I could tell his behavior was making Marisol uncomfortable."

"Is it possible you may be overreacting a bit?" I mean, I know you're under a lot of stress."

"Maybe your right," I replied. "I'll see how things go the rest of the week and will let you know if I experience any more issues."

After hanging up with Logan, I started reviewing email, but before I could respond to the first one, Dr. Taylor, the new Chancellor, summoned me to her office.

"I trust things went well with your mother?" She asked, reading a form in her hand, and avoiding eye contact.

"As well as can be expected, thanks for asking."

"Have you decided which day of the week to work remotely?"

"Yes, Wednesdays, so I can take Mom to her chemo appointments."

"Great. So, just to be clear, you're working remotely tomorrow, right?"

"Right."

After confirming I would be working remotely the next day, Dr. Taylor's eyes lit up like a Christmas tree as she abruptly changed the subject and started going on and on about Michael. She talked about the tremendous job he did while I was away, how knowledgeable he was, how impressed she was, how professional he was, and so on. As she continued laying it on thick and swooning over all things Michael, I literally threw up in my mouth. Still, I was grateful for the week I had off, and glad Michael impressed her while I was away.

Though I tried not to show it, the month following mom's cancer diagnosis was particularly difficult for me. Mom was fighting for her life with chemo and every Wednesday I was by her side, doing my best to keep her encouraged, and trying not to show how worried I really was. Ever since she started chemo, she was vomiting all the time, rapidly losing weight, and even losing her hair. And as if those side effects weren't bad enough, the chemo was changing her skin color from beautiful caramel to a dull, pale brown, and causing painful neuropathy in her hands. I was afraid for mom, so very afraid. The quality of her life was deteriorating before my eyes, and there wasn't a damn thing I could do to stop it.

In November 2016, Dr. Taylor hired Christine Shaw as the new Director of Enrollments at the Temple campus. Christine was a big-boned woman in her early thirties with warm butterscotch skin, crystal blue eyes, full red lips, and thick, curly black hair. She wore dresses that complimented her figure, three-inch designer pumps, and a beautiful gold locket with a picture of her Black mother on one side, and her White father on the other.

Christine was my counterpart at the Temple campus, and we instantly became good friends. And even though no one else realized she was half Black, I knew, and it felt good having another Black person on the management team.

After Dr. Taylor called a brief meeting in the conference room to introduce Christine to campus management, I returned to my office and received a call from mom.

"Hey," Mom said, tiredly. "Did Gabby tell ya 'bout my blood transfusion tomorrow?"

According to Gabrielle, mom's doctor said she needed a blood transfusion because her white blood cell count was too low, putting her at a higher risk of getting an infection which would be dangerous in her condition. He said the blood transfusion was needed to increase mom's white blood cell count.

"Yeah, she told me," I replied. "I'm gonna take you to your appointment."

"That's great, honey. Now finish workin' and I'll catch up with ya later. Love ya."

"Love you too, mom."

The next day, I took Mom to the outpatient clinic to get her blood transfusion, and after giving her a kiss on the cheek and the biggest bear hug imaginable, I stood there, watching with intensity, as the clinic staff member wheeled Mom away. I strained my eyes trying to see Mom for as long as I could, as she was wheeled down the corridor, and when she vanished from my sight, I gasped out loud as the memory of what happened the last time Mom was wheeled away frightened me.

"Jesus," I whispered before collapsing into my chair, and burying my face into both hands as teardrops covered my palms and soaked my cheeks.

I must've cried myself to sleep in that chair because an hour later, I awoke, squinting my eyes, and using my hand to block the hot sun beating down on my face through a window. Thankfully, an hour and a half later, Mom was wheeled back to me safe and sound, and I let out a deep sigh of relief.

After the blood transfusion, I took Mom to my house to recover while I kept an eye on her. That night, she slept like a baby, thank goodness, and the next day, my son and I waited on Mom hand and foot, ensuring that all her needs were met. We also watched a few of mom's favorite shows with her while she laid on the couch with the tube from her portable oxygen tank in her nose, and throwing up almost every hour in the bucket I had put next to the couch.

The next day, I made everyone breakfast and, thankfully, Mom was able to keep most of it down. Afterwards, I gave her a gentle sponge bath, and was careful when I washed the loose skin hanging from her thighs because it was very tender. And after helping Mom get dressed, I wheeled her to the car in her wheelchair, and spent the next couple of hours driving around the city, something she really wanted to do. And although we had to pull over on the side of the road a few times so she could throw up, we still had a great time together.

When I returned to work on Monday, I discovered that Paul Brown, the Corporate Vice President of Enrollments, was at the Temple campus training Christine Shaw. Paul, a man in his early forties, was the epitome of the perfect man. He was very attractive with short, blonde hair styled with mousse, creamy, vanilla skin as smooth as polished gems, captivating greenish-blue eyes, and a perfectly chiseled body and height. He wore custom made suits with designer jewelry, looked like he stepped off the cover of a fashion magazine, and had a scent and air about him that women and men alike were drawn to.

As Paul conducted his training in the conference room, I was in my office, behind closed doors, feeling my faith unravel as the heavy weight of mom's illness crushed me underneath. As each hour passed, I sank deeper into depression, as I fixated on the pair of scissors sitting on my desk. Then, my mind began to wander, and I imagined using the scissors to slit my wrists, permanently ending my pain.

For the next hour, I sat in a catatonic state embracing the darkness once more, and visualizing how I could use each object on my desk, from the stapler to the paper clip, as a tool to bring about my own destruction. Suddenly, there was a knock at my door, saving me from my suicidal ideation. It was Paul, who had taken a break from training to congratulate me on the awards I won. He was looking at me, and smiling as he peeked through the glass, but his smile turned into a frown when my swollen eyes met his, and before I knew it, he had opened the unlocked door, walked in, and was standing in front of my desk.

"Are you alright?" He asked, furrowing his plucked brows as he looked at me.

I couldn't bring myself to say one word. I just looked away, shaking my head as tears cascaded down my cheeks.

Then, in a stunning display of compassion, Paul walked around my desk, kneeled on the floor next to me, and placed his uncalloused hand on top of mine.

"Tell me what's wrong," he said, with a look of genuine sincerity.

I don't know if it was his compassionate nature, genuine concern, or act of placing his hand on top of mine the way Mom always did that touched me the most, but I completely broke down and unloaded everything I was feeling about mom, the colon cancer, the chemo side effects, and, most of all, my fear of losing mom.

Paul listened to me. He really listened.

"There may be something I can do to help," he said, giving my hand a few friendly pats. "I'll be in touch."

After Paul left, I closed my eyes, put my hands together in my lap, and thanked God for sending such a kindhearted and unexpected person to rescue me from the darkness, and restore my faith. I wasn't sure what he could do to help, but really appreciated having someone outside my family to talk to.

On the morning of Friday, December 30, 2016, I received the most amazing email from my boss, Logan.

From: MacDougal, Logan
Sent: Friday, December 30, 2016 9:50 AM
To: Ardoin, Ebony
Subject: Way to go!

Can't believe another year is in the books, Ebony. This was an excellent year for your department and a spectacular year for our campus. You were a key contributor to our success, if not the key contributor, and I'm excited to see more greatness from you in 2017!
Let me know if you want to pump some iron to celebrate!
Logan

When I read Logan's email, I had a smile on my face that was a mile wide, and I couldn't think of a better way to end the year.

As I continued working in my office, I took a few moments to reflect back on my career and was amazed by how far I came from the day my temp assignment as the Secretary began almost five years ago. And as I thought about my future at Daebrun, I felt happy and satisfied.

But later that afternoon, Dr. Taylor summoned me to her office for an impromptu meeting, and the happiness and satisfaction I felt earlier was replaced with nervousness and anxiety.

When I arrived at her office, she motioned me to have a seat. So, I walked in, closed the door behind me, and sat down in the chair in front of her desk.

"I trust you have big plans for the holiday?" She asked, sitting at her desk with both hands folded on top, and void of any emotion.

"Just planning to spend some much-needed time with my family," I replied. "Do you have big plans for the weekend?"

"Yes," she responded, with eyes as dark as two blackholes, and a face still void of emotion.

Then, she unfolded her hands, and pushed up the reading glasses she was wearing with her long, bony finger. And as she continued looking at me, I saw a burst of excitement in her eyes as the pleasantries were abruptly cut short, and she dropped a bombshell that brought my fear of racism barreling back to the forefront.

"Listen, Ebony," she said, leaning back in her chair and almost salivating with glee, "Michael's going to start attending the SF Leadership Calls in your place from now on."

In my place? I thought to myself. *Yeah, I don't think so.*

"Thanks, but that isn't necessary," I politely said. "The conference calls are on Thursdays when I'm on campus, so there's no need for him to attend in my place."

Dr. Taylor stared at me and pursed her lips together so tight they started turning blue. After a few seconds, she took a deep breath.

"Read between the lines, Ebony. I'm going to promote you to Senior Director soon. Michael needs management exposure, so he can replace you as Director. Understand?"

Not only did I *not* understand, but I was also suspicious of her motives for wanting to promote Michael. There was another employee on my team, Marisol, who had seniority and was better qualified. And why was she so interested in my department all of a sudden? I didn't even report to her, I reported to Logan. And where was Logan? Why wasn't he present while this information was being communicated to me?

"A promotion would be great," I said, trying to remain calm. "Michael and I can attend the call together."

Suddenly, Dr. Taylor leaped from her chair like she was possessed by a demon, leaned over her desk with both palms lying flat, and roared, spraying spit across her desk with each word, "Are you deaf? I said you are not to be on that call!"

As she stood there glaring at me with big, bulging eyes, I was shaking in my seat. And as I wiped her spit from my face, I was afraid she was going to hurl green, projectile vomit at me.

A couple of minutes later, Dr. Taylor sat back down, ran both hands across her stringy hair to make sure her bun was still in place, then dropped *another* bombshell that shocked me even more than the first one.

"You are *not* to have any further contact with Corporate and if anyone contacts you, I expect to be notified."

Then, before I could respond, she rudely dismissed me from her office.

As I walked back to my office, I was appalled, and kicked myself repeatedly for not trusting my original instincts. Dr. Taylor wasn't just another racist. She was an evil woman who used mom's cancer diagnosis as the spark to set in motion her plan to derail my career, and replace me as the leader of the Student Finance department with Michael, not because he was more qualified, but because he was White.

When I returned to my office, I documented the gut-wrenching conversation with Dr. Taylor in my Daily Log, and sent the following email recapping our conversation:

From: Ardoin, Ebony
Sent: Friday, December 30, 2016 4:03 PM
To: Taylor, Karen
Subject: Meeting Recap

Dear Dr. Taylor,

Just a quick note to recap the conversation we had in your office a few minutes ago. It is my understanding that you want Michael Sullivan, my employee, to start attending the SF Leadership Calls in my place, effective immediately. You stated that you are planning to promote me to Senior Director soon and would like Michael to gain management exposure to replace me as Director when I'm promoted.

It is also my understanding you want me to discontinue contacting Corporate, and to notify you if I am contacted.

Please let me know if my understanding is incorrect.

Sincerely,

Ebony Ardoin, Director of Student Finance

After the email was sent, I saved it on the free online storage website I was using. I never received a response from Dr. Taylor, but it didn't matter. The email was evidence I could use to not only prove I was being prevented from performing my job duties, but also that I was forced to assign my duties to my White employee.

I was too upset to continue working, so I left and began my commute back home to begin what should've been a wonderful three-day holiday weekend. As I drove, I replayed everything that occurred that day in my head, and wondered if the amazing email I had received from Logan that morning was actually some kind of hidden mea culpa for what he knew was going to happen to me that afternoon. The only thing that gave me a slight, and oddly weird, bit of comfort was the notion that things, both personally and professionally, could not get any worse…or so I thought.

CHAPTER 9

The Mother of All Retaliations

In January 2017, I returned to work after the holiday weekend with a heavy heart, and reluctantly sent the email to Michael Sullivan, my White employee, providing him with the SF Leadership Call dial-in information, and instructing him to begin attending in my place, per Dr. Taylor's directive. Afterwards, I saved a copy of the email as more evidence proving that I was not only being prevented from performing my duties, but also that my duties were being assigned to my White employee.

The next day, Michael began attending the SF Leadership Calls, and the only way I could learn about the information conveyed by Corporate during the calls, was to debrief him, which was beyond humiliating. And, as if that wasn't bad enough, Michael was in Dr. Taylor's office for hours on end each day, talking about or doing God only knows what.

As each day passed, it became crystal clear that Michael was fully aware of Dr. Taylor's plan to promote him to my position after derailing my career, because he lost all respect for me as the leader of the Student Finance department, and stopped doing a great deal of his work. So, to keep the department from reverting back to the disaster I inherited, I picked up the slack on top of everything else I was dealing with, and worked seventy to eighty hours a week keeping the department running smoothly.

In February 2017, Corporate announced that the annual federal audit was going to be conducted again in the Student Finance department at all Daebrun campuses beginning the following week. The federal audit covered fiscal year 2016, which ran from January 1st through December 31st of that year.

As you may recall, the last federal audit that occurred at the Temple campus covered fiscal year 2015, and the results were disastrous. We received a whopping nine audit findings, which put the campus at risk of losing its eligibility to participate in the federal financial aid programs. Since the majority of Temple students used federal financial aid to pay most, if not all, of their educational costs, Corporate would have no choice but to close the campus if we lost the ability to offer it. And because this audit covered the period during which I was the leader, the stakes were high, and I knew if I didn't successfully pass the audit this time, I could kiss my job goodbye.

The team of auditors arrived at the Temple campus a week later and, just like before, spent the entire week auditing everything in my department from A to Z. But unlike the last time they audited my department, I wasn't a nervous wreck. I was calm and confident because I trusted the processes I developed and implemented that year. And when the lead auditor conducted her exit meeting at the end of the week with me, Dr. Taylor, my boss Logan, and Aaron Burns, the Chief Student Finance Officer at Corporate (who was on speaker phone), she congratulated me on the "miraculous" job I did in not only resolving all nine findings from the previous audit, but also not incurring any new findings. Aaron Burns was ecstatic!

"Ebony, do you know what this means?" He exclaimed, after hearing the news.

"It means we did a great job," I replied, smiling like I had just discovered gold.

"Oh, it means a lot more than that," Aaron continued. "This is the first time, in the history of Daebrun, that a campus made it through a federal audit with zero audit findings! Congratulations on a job well done!"

"Yes, Ebony, *the SF Team* did a tremendous job," Dr. Taylor said, as she subtly tried to shift Aaron's focus from *me* doing a great job to the "SF team" doing a great job.

After the meeting ended, Aaron sent a mass email announcement to the Chancellors and Student Finance teams, at all seventy campuses owned by Corporate, announcing the good news and congratulating me on producing such impressive results. After reading his email, I saved it as evidence because it proved that I performed my job at a very high level. I also saved the audit report from the previous year, when the audit results were a disaster, to show how bad things were before I became the leader.

Two weeks later, I received a cryptic phone call. It was Paul Brown, the Corporate Vice President of Enrollments. As you may recall, he was the attractive man who rescued me from my suicidal thoughts two months prior when he stopped by my office unexpectedly.

"Ebony, I need you to drop what you're doing, and join me on an urgent conference call already in progress," he sternly said.

"Uh, ok no problem," I nervously replied.

Then, he provided me with the conference call dial-in instructions. I had no idea what the call was about but figured maybe a student or parent was upset and had contacted Corporate.

When I dialed in to the conference call, a male voice on the other end of the phone said, "Ebony, thank you for joining us. Do you know who this is?"

"Yes, I recognize your voice. This is Aaron Burns, right?" I asked, wondering what the heck was going on.

"Yes, it is," he said, with a light-hearted chuckle. "Also, on the call with us are Paul Brown and Dr. Taylor. We are all big fans of yours and are aware of the situation with your mother. She lives in Austin, right?"

"Yes, that's correct," I replied, not knowing where the conversation was going.

Then Aaron said something that almost knocked me off my chair and onto the floor.

"Because of your excellent job performance, and the situation with your mother, I've been authorized to offer you the National Director of SF promotion previously held by Kyle Charron."

When I heard this news, my heart skipped a beat. Was I really being promoted again?

"If you accept this promotion," Aaron continued, "you'll be transferred back to the Austin campus, allowing you to be closer to your sick mother, and you can oversee operations at the Temple campus remotely."

Normally, I would *never* have considered going back to the Austin campus, especially after everything I'd been through. But with Ms. Kelly, Malcolm Webb, *and* Kyle Charron gone, transferring back to the Austin campus sounded like a dream come true, because I wanted to work in the same city as mom, and also get the hell away from Dr. Taylor.

"Do you need time to think before accepting this promotion?" He asked.

"No. I'm definitely interested," I said excitedly, "and grateful to everyone on this call for making it possible."

Aaron then instructed me to call Amanda Ross, the Chancellor at the Austin campus, to schedule a date and time to review the specifics of the National Director position, and after I thanked everyone again for their support, the call ended, and I documented the details of the call in my Daily Log.

Although Dr. Taylor avoided all contact with me for the rest of the day, I imagined she was just as excited about the National Director promotion as I was. Afterall, with me transferring to Austin, she could promote Michael to Director of Student Finance in Temple, and finally have the White person she wanted in my position.

Before I left work, I sent an email to Dr. Taylor thanking her for her support. I never received a response. I also sent the following email to both Paul Brown and Aaron Burns:

From: Ardoin, Ebony
Sent: Tuesday, February 21, 2017 11:31 AM
To: Burns, Aaron; Brown, Paul
Subject: Thank you so much!

Dear Aaron and Paul,

Just a quick note to thank you for the National Director of Student Finance promotion! I am so grateful for the opportunity to transfer back to the Austin campus and work in the same city that my mom lives as she deals with cancer.

I spoke with Amanda Ross, the Chancellor in Austin, a few minutes ago, and scheduled the meeting next week to review the specifics of the National Director position.

Then, I saved copies of both emails as proof that I was offered the National Director of Student Finance promotion.

On my way home that evening, I thanked God for the blessings I had received, and for making it possible for me to escape from Dr. Taylor's evil clutches. After months of agonizing turmoil and stress, things were finally taking a turn for the better.

When I arrived at work the next day, I was in good spirit and excited about transitioning to the National Director position at the Austin campus. But immediately after I sat down at my desk to begin my day, I received a call from Dr. Taylor summoning me to her office. When I got there, I wasn't the least bit surprised to see Michael, sitting in her office when he should've been sitting in his cubicle working. I was tired of Michael taking advantage of Dr. Taylor's preferential treatment and was thrilled I wouldn't have to deal with him, or her, for too much longer.

When Dr. Taylor noticed me standing in her doorway, she motioned Michael to leave as I walked in. As he stood up and walked towards me, he flashed me a fake smile and said, "Congratulations, Ebony." Then, I heard him snickering as he left and closed the door behind him.

As I walked over and sat down in front of her desk, I noticed that her normally pale cheeks were flush from what appeared to be either anger, or a heightened state of arousal from having Michael in her office.

"What's going on?" I asked.

"I consider myself to be a reasonable woman," she said, her eyes full of rage and laser focused on me. "I ordered you not to contact anyone at Corporate, and I expected that order to be obeyed."

Suddenly, it dawned on me. Dr. Taylor was angry about the conversation I had with Paul Brown that resulted in the National Director promotion I was offered.

"I didn't contact Paul if that's what you're thinking. He sought me out before you issued your no contact directive."

"And when he did, you whined about your poor, sick mother in Austin!" She said, banging her fists on her desk and causing her empty coffee mug to fall over. "You should've reported your little chat to me immediately instead of letting me get blindsided!"

"You being blindsided has nothing to do with me," I boldly said, leaning back in my chair as I crossed my legs.

"It has everything to do with you!" She snarled, spraying spit across the desk once again that, thankfully, missed my face this time. "You made him believe you were going to quit if he didn't do something!"

At this point, I was feeling threatened, and worried about the situation escalating and having a negative effect on my promotion.

"Umm, I think I should leave," I calmly said, as I stood up.

"Ebony, wait," she replied, abruptly. "I'm just trying to help you. You left Austin to get away from the wolves, right?"

"True. And since you know that I'm sure you also know that the wolves I had problems with are gone now."

Dr. Taylor locked eyes with me, leaned forward, and whispered something that sent an eerie chill down my spine. "But their pups are still there, and they're very hungry."

"What is that supposed to mean?" I replied, as I sat in my chair speechless, and staring back at her.

She didn't respond. And after a few minutes of awkward silence, Dr. Taylor sternly said, "Well, if you are hell-bent on accepting that promotion, you need to get Michael ready to replace you. This campus will not fall because of your decision."

The following week, I went to the Austin campus and met with Amanda Ross, the Chancellor, regarding the National Director of Student Finance promotion.

"Your role as the National Director will be to groom Latoya into the leader I know she can be. I like her, and she's doing a fairly decent job, but her department is struggling, mostly because her team doesn't respect her."

"Okay, I can do that."

"I want you to provide her, and her team, with training, tools, and direction," she said. "You know, Kyle's job done the right way."

Amanda further explained that my transfer back to the Austin campus would occur in three weeks, per Dr. Taylor's request, to give me time to train my replacement in Temple. She also explained that my annual salary of sixty-six thousand dollars would be paid by both campuses in equal shares, although my paycheck would be issued in Austin.

Immediately after my meeting, I emailed Amanda a recap of everything we discussed, and copied Aaron Burns and Dr. Taylor. Then, I saved a copy of the email as evidence that proved I was offered the National Director promotion with a salary of sixty-six thousand dollars a year.

As I drove home from the Austin campus, I was on cloud nine and couldn't believe it! Not only was it going to be easier to see Mom during the week, but my salary was also going to increase to a whopping sixty-six thousand dollars a year! I was so excited and couldn't wait to tell Mom the good news, so I stopped by her apartment. When I got there, she was laying in her bed watching one of her favorite shows, and when I shared the good news with her, she was just as excited as I was.

"What a blessin' for you *and* me," she said, looking at me with tired eyes. "God is good."

The next day, I went back to work, and Marisol poked her head into my office.

"Boss, can I speak with you?"

"Sure, come on in."

Marisol walked in and closed the door behind her.

"Boss, what's going on? First, you put Michael in charge when I been here seven years and he's only been here two years."

"Oh, Mari, I'm so sorry," I sadly said, as my eyes teared up. "I told Logan to put you in charge when I was in the hospital with mom, but Dr. Taylor went behind me and put Michael in charge."

Marisol's eyes filled up with tears. "Okay so now, Michael says your leaving and he's getting your job. Is that true?"

When she asked her question, I got a huge lump inside my throat, and felt so bad for her.

"I was promoted to National Director in Austin, Mari. I was going to tell you and Michael after everything was finalized, but it sounds like Dr. Taylor already told him. And sadly, yes. Dr. Taylor is promoting

Michael to my position. She wouldn't let me choose. Again, I'm so sorry."

"You don't have to be sorry, boss. It's not your fault. He got your job 'cause he's a gringo. That's just the way it is."

Then, she got up, gave me a little hug, and walked out, and I felt awful. Just awful.

An hour later, Michael came to my office, and I began training him and getting him ready to replace me as the Director of Student Finance in Temple. But an hour after we began, I received a desperate phone call from Amanda Ross at the Austin campus.

"I know your Mom is sick, and your promotion hasn't been finalized yet, but I really need your help," she said, worriedly. "The federal auditors will be here next week, and I'm *very* concerned about the condition of our files."

Then, Amanda asked if I would be willing to work at her campus over the weekend to audit her team's files and direct them on how to get them cleaned up before Latoya received the sample list of students from the lead auditor on Monday morning.

"I know it's asking a lot," she said. "But I would be grateful, and on the bright side reviewing our files will give you a head start in your role as National Director."

Amanda's request was quite extraordinary. Not only did she want me to give up my weekend with my family on such short notice, but she also wanted me to work at her campus before my promotion was finalized and before my salary was increased.

Under normal circumstances I would've respectfully declined, but since my promotion was taking effect in a few weeks, and I was going to be responsible for the success of her Student Finance department anyway, I said yes.

That weekend, instead of spending precious time with my family, I went to the Austin campus to help Latoya and her team.

"Hey, girl!" Latoya exclaimed as she gave me a big hug. "I'm so happy to see you!"

After we spent a few minutes exchanging pleasantries, Latoya said something that really bothered me.

"I miss hearing you on the leadership call. You so good, you don't have to attend anymore?"

79

"I was told *not* to attend." I replied, fighting the temptation to say I was told not to attend by a racist piece of shit.

"Well, you're the only one from Daebrun that's not attending," she said, with a friendly laugh.

After Latoya's comments, my blood was boiling on the inside as the reminder that I was being discriminated against by Dr. Taylor hit me like a speeding car. On the outside, though, I remained professional and helped Latoya and her team prepare for the upcoming audit. For twelve hours on Saturday and twelve on Sunday, I audited their files and directed them on how to resolve the issues, and by weekend's end, I was completely worn out, but at least their files were in proper order, and I felt good about the progress we made.

The next morning, as I was driving to the Temple campus, I received a call on my cell phone. It was Amanda, the Chancellor at the Austin campus.

"Ebony, I'm sorry to be the bearer of bad news," she said, "but I just found out the National Director position has been eliminated."

"Oh my God!" I exclaimed, as a surge of shock overtook me, and I almost hit a car in the other lane. "What happened?"

"I don't know all the details," she said, "but apparently Dr. Taylor contacted Dr. Gershon, our CEO, and made a huge deal about how Corporate blindsided her with your promotion, and how her campus will suffer without you managing it full-time."

I pulled over to the side of the road and sat, with my mouth gaping open, in a state of suspended disbelief, as it hit me that Dr. Taylor was literally holding me hostage at the Temple campus, and retaliating against me for accepting the National Director promotion. But she didn't just retaliate, what she did was the mother of all retaliations. By blocking my promotion, she not only ruined any chance I had of getting away from her with my job and dignity still intact, but she also destroyed my chance of working in the same city as my gravely ill mom, who was already living on borrowed time.

As I continued driving to the Temple campus, I was in despair as I imagined Dr. Taylor and Michael, sitting in her office giving each other high five's and swapping spit behind closed doors, as Dr. Taylor bragged about how she blocked my promotion after I worked at the Austin campus for free. And as my mind raced with torturous thoughts of Dr. Taylor and Michael laughing it up, I cried until I didn't have any tears left.

When I arrived at work, my plan was to avoid all human contact until I could pull myself together, but as soon as I arrived, I saw Dr. Taylor. She was standing at the reception desk in the lobby waiting for me, and as I approached the entrance to the campus, I got a bad taste in my mouth.

"I just got off the phone with Amanda," she said, opening her eyes wide and putting her hands together. "I know you're upset, but I did it for your own good. You'll thank me later."

I didn't say a word, mostly because there was a big lump in my throat, and I knew I had been defeated. So, I stood there silently with my purse hanging on my shoulder and with heavy, tear-filled eyes.

"On a positive note, I have some news I think will make your day," she said. "Come with me."

As she walked away, I trailed slowly behind her, and when we were inside her office, she closed the door, walked over, and sat down at her desk as I slowly sat down in the chair in front of her desk.

"I was going to wait until tomorrow to give you your performance review," she said. "But I'll give it to you now."

Great, I thought to myself. *Go ahead and kick me while I'm down.*

Then, she reached into her desk, pulled out two copies of my performance review, and handed one copy to me, and as she reviewed each section, I was thoroughly confused. For whatever reason, she gave me a spectacular review, and rated me as 'Frequently Exceeds Expectations', the highest rating possible. She even went through the trouble of listing my accomplishments and wrote paragraph after paragraph singing my praises stating how amazing I was as the leader of the Student Finance department. She ended the performance review with a written statement that said, "I am giving Ebony a twenty percent raise and promoting her to Senior Director of Student Finance, effective immediately. Her new annual salary is sixty-six thousand dollars."

When I read the sentence stating that I was going to receive the same salary I would've received as the National Director of Student Finance, my jaw dropped to the floor.

"It wasn't easy getting approval to offer you the same salary you were going to get as the National Director, but I was willing to fight for you," Dr. Taylor said. "I blocked your promotion because I value you, and don't want to share you with another campus. Understand?"

"Yes. Thank you," I replied in a low voice.

Then Dr. Taylor said she knew we had rocky beginnings and recommended that we put the past behind us and start fresh. She also promised to support me better if I continued supporting her and offered me her right hand to shake.

"Sounds like a good plan." I said as we shook hands and sealed the deal. "So, do I report to you now, or is Logan still my boss?" I asked.

"You still report to Logan, but you have a strong dotted line to me."

Immediately after I left Dr. Taylor's office, she sent an email announcing my promotion to all staff at the Temple campus.

From: Taylor, Karen
Sent: Monday, March 06, 2017 9:44 AM
To: @DAEBRUN-TEM Staff
Subject: Organizational Announcement

Colleagues:

I am thrilled to announce the promotion of Ebony Ardoin to Senior Director of Student Finance, effective immediately. Ebony has done a spectacular job managing all areas of Student Finance and has been a valued asset to our campus.

Please join me in congratulating Ebony on her well-deserved promotion.

Karen Taylor, Ph.D.
Chancellor

The loss of the National Director promotion was a devastating blow, but there was an unexpected silver lining. Much to my surprise, Dr. Taylor gave me an outstanding performance review, promoted me to Senior Director of Student Finance, and increased my annual salary to sixty-six thousand dollars!

After saving a copy of my performance review as proof of my outstanding performance, promotion, and new salary, and the email Dr. Taylor sent announcing my promotion, I sat in my office and reflected on my last five years of employment. It was at that moment that I realized it was through the adversity of racism that my relationship with Jesus began, and my faith in God grew. And while I still didn't trust Dr. Taylor in any way, shape, or form, she put her racist tendencies aside for the greater good of the campus, finally accepted me as the leader of the Student Finance department, and now there was nothing standing in my way up the ladder to success...or so I thought.

CHAPTER 10

Are Your Braids Too Tight?

After my promotion to Senior Director of Student Finance took effect, my confidence as the leader of my department was restored. And as I reclaimed the authority vested in me by my title, my first official act was to notify Michael that I would be attending the SF Leadership Calls moving forward, and his attendance on the calls was no longer required. After calling him to my office, I gave him a friendly greeting and motioned him to have a seat.

"Thank you for attending the leadership calls in my place over the last few months," I said.

"No problem," he responded, looking down at his cell phone.

"I'll be attending the calls from now on, so you'll get that hour back in your day to work on other things."

When he heard the news, he looked up and gave me a smug smirk.

"Does Dr. Taylor know?" He asked, crossing his arms, and glaring at me.

"The important thing is that *you* know," I replied. "Do you have any other questions?"

He didn't say a word. He just jumped up, muttered something under his breath, and stomped out of my office.

Three days later, I dialed in for the first SF Leadership Call I had attended in months, and it felt good to be back in the driver's seat. I had only been on the call for fifteen minutes, though, when Dr. Taylor showed up unannounced and tried to open my closed door. But when she discovered the door was locked, and realized the element of surprise was over, she jiggled the doorknob frustratingly and banged on the glass, motioning me to let her in.

When I opened the door, she walked past me without saying a word, and headed straight for my desk. Then, she stood as stiff as a bony statue for several seconds staring at my desk and listening to the leadership call that I had on speaker phone.

"Is that the leadership call?" She asked, sounding irritated.

"Yes," I said with confidence, determined not to walk on eggshells around her anymore.

I don't know if she was shocked by my confidence or just had a lack of words, but instead of causing a scene, which I fully expected her to do, she glared at me for a few moments while shaking her head, then turned around and walked out. And I, determined not to be deterred by her theatrics, remained on the leadership call until the very end.

Immediately after I hung up, my desk phone rang. It was Steve Burger, the Corporate Director of Student Finance, who visited me a year ago to assess operations after my department almost failed my first federal audit.

"I was glad to hear your voice on the call today," he said. "I was under the impression you had moved on to greener pastures."

"No, the pastures are green enough here," I said, with a smile I'm sure he felt through the phone. "Just had a lot going on the last few months. Is there something I can do for you?"

"We're in the planning phase of the annual Directors of Student Finance Conference to be held in Las Vegas later this year. We're expecting at least seventy participants from all campuses and I'm in charge of selecting presenters who are at the top of their game. You have been selected."

When I heard this news, I was thrilled. Being selected to present at a training conference was not only a huge honor, but it was also a very big deal. Only people who Corporate viewed as experts were selected to share their leadership, knowledge, and presentation skills, so presenting at this conference had the potential to catapult my career. And although Mom was very sick, I knew she wouldn't want me to miss this rare opportunity.

"Wow, what an honor!" I exclaimed. "I'd be delighted!"

"Your role will be to prepare a presentation on identifying and monitoring the repack population, and then train the conference attendees during your designated breakout session."

The repack population was a term used in student finance circles to describe the population of students whose current financial aid packages were on the verge of expiring.

After we hung up, I sent a courtesy email to Logan giving him the great news and copied Dr. Taylor. Five minutes later, Dr. Taylor stormed into my office, slamming the door shut with her long, spindly arm.

"Are your braids too tight?" She yelled, almost foaming at the mouth. "What part of do not have any contact with corporate do you not understand?"

"I don't understand why you're upset," I replied. "This is an amazing growth opportunity for me, and a huge visibility opportunity for this campus."

"What you understand doesn't really matter, now does it?" She said, snapping back at me.

Then her eyes widened in an eerie sort of way, and I could see the wheels turning in her head.

"Tell you what. I'll think about it," she calmly said. "But I want an email directly from the source explaining why they need *you* specifically, before I'll commit to anything. *And* I did not give you permission to start attending those calls again, so stop until I tell you otherwise."

Then she stormed out of my office as quickly as she stormed in.

It was at that moment that I realized her speech about us having a fresh start and supporting me better was just a bunch of B.S. and nothing had changed. She was still discriminating against me and preventing me from doing my job.

After she left, I documented the conversation in my Daily Log. Then, I called Steve Burger.

"Dr. Taylor won't authorize me to participate until she receives an email from you explaining the reason my participation is necessary."

"That's weird," he replied. "Normally, Chancellors are excited to find out someone from their campus has been selected."

An hour later, he sent an email to Dr. Taylor, as she requested, and copied me.

When I received Steve's email, I saved it as evidence because it proved that I was an expert in my field and a valuable asset.

Although Steve sent Dr. Taylor the email she requested immediately, one week went by and she had not responded. Concerned, Steve sent a follow-up email to Dr. Taylor and requested a status update. Another week passed and, again, there was no response.

In April 2017, things began spiraling downward fast as Dr. Taylor ramped up her efforts to derail my career and replace me with Michael. It started with her response to Steve Burger's email, which she sent more than two weeks after he requested my participation as a presenter at the Directors of Student Finance Conference.

Steve:

Thank you for your patience while I considered your request for Ms. Ardoin to present at this year's DSF Conference. While I agree that Ms. Ardoin is a valued asset to the SF world, she is also a valued asset at my campus. Due to several initiatives we are working on, and the cancer diagnosis of her mother, the timing is such that I cannot, in good conscience, authorize Ms. Ardoin to participate.

As an alternative, I have approved Michael Sullivan to present at the conference in Ms. Ardoin's place. Mr. Sullivan is knowledgeable in all areas of student finance and will represent our campus well.

Please reach out to him at your earliest convenience to discuss logistics. I included him on this email to loop him in.

Thanks,

Karen Taylor, Ph.D.

Chancellor

When I received her response in my inbox, I threw my hands up in anger and almost had a massive coronary. Not only did Dr. Taylor use *mom's* cancer diagnosis as justification to choke away yet another opportunity I had for growth, but she also gave my golden opportunity to present at the DSF conference to Michael, of all people, adding insult to injury. I wanted to cry but forced the tears back, and instead took comfort in reminding myself that her cruel email was more evidence I needed to prove racial discrimination. Then, as always, I saved the email.

As I sat in my office suffering in dumb anguish, I received a perfectly timed call from mom.

"Somethin' told me to call ya," Mom said, sounding weak. "You ok, child?"

When I was growing up, Mom and I joked about having a psychic connection with each other because we always seemed to know when something was wrong.

"Oh mom," I cried out, no longer able to hold back the tears. "Things are really bad here, and I wanna quit so bad. I know the money's great, but is it worth the pain and suffering?"

"Listen. I know I told ya before not to make waves, but I was wrong. I had a dream," Mom said. "I saw ya fightin' and standin' your ground, and you were wearing the armor of God. And when the battle was over, victory was yours, honey."

"I won't give up, mom," I said with a sigh. "I'll keep fighting."

"And as long as there's breath in my body, I'll keep prayin' for ya," Mom replied.

Two weeks later, while I was with Mom at her chemo appointment, I received a voice message from Logan that was odd because he had barely interacted with me since last December.

"I need you to email me the process documentation for your department," he said.

I didn't trust Logan as far as I could throw him anymore, suspected he was in cahoots with Dr. Taylor, and firmly believed that he wanted my process documentation so he would have a blue print of how I managed my department, before Dr. Taylor destroyed my career and fired me. So, I temporarily ignored the voice message and decided to wait until I was back in the office to speak with him, in person, and try to get a read on him.

When I returned to work the next day, and before I had an opportunity to reach out to Logan regarding his request, I received *another* request, this time in the form of an email from Travis Clayton, the National Director of Human Resources at the Austin campus, who replaced Amanda Ross after she was promoted to Chancellor. Travis was a muscle-bound man in his late twenties with an average height, and mesmerizing green eyes. He had fair skin with a pink hue, freckles scattered across his nose and cheeks, and strawberry-blonde hair with a five o'clock shadow. He wore tight dress pants with fitted dress shirts, carried a gallon of water everywhere he went, and prided himself on being the ultimate gym rat.

His email said that Amanda Ross had asked him to reach out to me to request copies of the documentation I created for managing my department. Apparently, she wanted him to get my processes so she could use them to improve student finance operations at her campus.

When I received Travis' request, I was furious and couldn't believe that he had the nerve to ask. If I had been given the promotion to National Director of Student Finance like I was promised, the Austin campus wouldn't need to request my documentation because they'd already have it, my processes would've already been implemented, and their student finance operations would've already improved. Now, they wanted me to just hand over the results of my blood, tears, and sweat, no questions asked.

I found the timing of his request to be suspicious, as well. Was it possible that Travis and Amanda knew what Dr. Taylor was doing to me? Were they trying to get their hands on my documentation now, because they knew I wouldn't be around in the near future?

When I returned to the Temple campus the following day, Logan came to my office, and I met with him regarding his request to receive my process documentation.

"Just out of curiosity," I said. "What are you planning to do with it?"

"I'm going to use it as a guide in training the other department heads," he replied. "Once processes across all departments are documented, I'll work with compliance to create a master file for cross-training and coverage purposes."

His answer to my question made logical sense, and even though I still didn't want to comply, I really had no choice since anything I created as an Daebrun employee was considered their intellectual property, not mine. I also reluctantly sent my process documentation to Travis Clayton at the Austin campus, per his request.

On the morning of May 1, 2017, Dr. Taylor walked into my office closing the door behind her, sat down at my desk, and crossed her skinny legs.

"Michael is out of control," she said, with a concerned look on her face. "Logan told me that Michael thinks the information you require them to tell students who want to borrow extra student loans is unethical. Did you know that?"

"No," I replied. "This is the first time I've heard about him having any concerns."

"He's a good kid but he's immature," she said. "Anyway, I defended you. I told him the methods you have in place keep our default rate low. Do you see why I didn't want you to take the National position? If you left, this campus would suffer the consequences."

"Understood," I replied, trying not to get whiplash from her constant mood swings.

Then, Dr. Taylor urged me to deal with this situation before it got out of hand, and recommended that I debrief Logan right away.

After thanking her for the heads up, I returned to my office, called Logan, and asked him to share the details of his conversation with Michael to give me an opportunity to respond. Then, Logan said that Michael came to him a few weeks ago concerned about what we disclose to students who request to borrow extra student loan funds. He said Michael told him that he tried to speak with me regarding his concerns, but I ignored him.

"That's not true," I said, frustratingly. "I'm hearing about this for the first time."

Logan went on to say that according to Michael, I require him and Marisol to present the students with two figures: The total amount they're eligible to receive, and the total amount they need just to cover Daebrun's costs. Michael believed our process was unethical because it was different from other colleges he had previously worked at.

When Logan shared this information with me, I was fit to be tied. Why on earth did he keep his conversations with Michael a secret for three weeks? And why didn't he bring his concern to me? If he had, I would've happily shared with him that the process in question was not only aligned with Corporate policy but was also one of the processes reviewed and approved by Aaron Burns, the Chief Student Finance Officer, himself. And more importantly, it was one of the processes I used during fiscal year 2016 that resulted in zero audit findings for the first time in Daebrun history.

After speaking with Logan, I was extremely upset and needed to vent. So, I called Christine Shaw, the Director of Enrollments, and one of the only people at the Temple campus I believed I could trust. And after telling her about the disturbing situation that had unfolded between Michael and Logan, she became just as upset as I was.

"You know, they've been meeting in your office every Wednesday for the last month or so when you're working remotely," she said. "I didn't think much of it at the time 'cause I assumed you were aware."

What? I thought to myself as I became even more upset. Not only was Logan meeting with Michael behind my back, but he was doing it *in my office* and when he knew I would be away.

"No, I wasn't aware, and I don't know what's going on," I replied.

"You should try talking to Logan again. Maybe he doesn't realize that he's undermining you."

After hanging up, I decided to take Christine's advice and called Logan again. When he answered, I requested to meet with him in person to further discuss the information he shared with me about Michael. He was willing to meet and ten minutes later, he arrived at my office, walked in, and closed the door behind him. Then he sat down in front of my desk.

"Logan, you're my boss and I have the utmost respect for you. But I'm Michael's boss, and it concerns me that you have been meeting with him, about perceived issues in my department, undermining my position."

"I wasn't trying to undermine you. I was trying to help."

"If you had discussed his concerns with me, I would've happily shared with you that the process in question is not only aligned with Corporate policy, but was also reviewed *and* approved by Aaron Burns, the Chief Student Finance Officer at Corporate."

"You're right, Ebony," Logan said. "And I'm sorry. I should've come to you."

After thanking Logan for his apology and support, I schedule a meeting with Michael to clear the air, and requested Logan's attendance at the meeting to project a united front.

After meeting with Logan, I felt better about the situation. He handled my concerns with sincerity and professionalism, admitted his actions in undermining my position were wrong, and even apologized for his behavior. It also gave me a sense of comfort in knowing that Logan would be present during my meeting with Michael to discuss this situation. Michael's behavior had become so erratic and abrasive lately, and I believed having Logan by my side would help in getting Michael back on the right track…or so I thought.

Chapter 11

And Then There Were Three

The next day, Michael came to my office, with the usual scowl on his face, for the meeting to discuss his concerns about the process used in my department that he deemed unethical. But, when he walked in and saw Logan, the scowl immediately disappeared as he sat down. Then, I began the meeting.

"Michael, it's my understanding you have concerns about the process we use when students request to borrow extra student loan funds. Correct?"

"Yeah."

"Well, the process in question was created to adhere to the policy. So, in actuality, you're questioning the policy, right?"

"Right."

Then I explained to Michael that we don't create policies, Corporate does. Our responsibility is to create processes that adhere to those policies. I also explained that the process he took issue with was not only approved by Aaron Burns, the Chief Student Finance Officer at Corporate, but was also reviewed by the federal auditors. And finally, I reminded Michael that I have an open-door policy, and he should bring any questions or concerns regarding student finance operations to me to discuss.

"I get it," Michael said, sounding agreeable and sincere. "I'm sorry, and I'll come to you if I have any other questions."

After Michael left, Logan said he thought the meeting went well, and that he was proud of the way I diffused the situation.

93

After Logan left, I documented the conversation in my Daily Log, and sent Dr. Taylor and Logan an email, that I also saved as evidence, recapping everything that had occurred. Immediately after sending the email, I received a phone call from Dr. Taylor.

"I don't appreciate receiving emails from you to cover your butt. So, stop!"

Before I could respond, she hung up on me. Afterwards I documented the phone conversation in my Daily Log and sent the following email:

From: Ardoin, Ebony
Sent: Tuesday, May 02, 2017 11:33 AM
To: Taylor, Karen
Subject: Emails

Dear Dr. Taylor,

During our phone conversation a few minutes ago, you instructed me to stop sending you emails. This email is being sent to memorialize our discussion.

Please let me know if my understanding of your instructions is incorrect.

Sincerely,

Ebony Ardoin, Senior Director of Student Finance

I never received a response, but it didn't matter. Since sending emails was a core part of my duties, the email was more evidence proving that she was preventing me from doing my job.

Things at the Temple campus were relatively quiet for a week and appeared to be calming down and normalizing. But then, I received the following email from Michael:

From: Sullivan, Michael
Sent: Wednesday, May 10, 2017 12:03 PM
To: Ardoin, Ebony
Cc: Taylor, Karen; MacDougal, Logan

After receiving Michael's email, I went to his cubicle to speak with him, but he wasn't there. I also tried calling him on his cell phone, but he didn't answer. So, since he had copied Logan and Dr. Taylor on his email, I tried calling both of them at their office numbers, but neither one answered. I even tried reaching them on their cell phones and still there was no answer.

Forty minutes later, I received another email from Michael that was ice cold and to the point.

When I received his second email, I called his cell phone again, and this time he answered.

"What do you want, Ebony?" He rudely asked.

"You don't have to be rude, Michael. I'm calling to say I'm glad you rescinded your resignation. I tried to call you when I received your first email but couldn't reach you."

He didn't say a word.

"What happened that made you want to resign and then rescind your resignation?"

"Ask Dr. Taylor," he smugly said.

"Thanks for the update and again I'm glad you're staying."

Michael didn't respond, he simply hung up in my face.

Afterwards, I immediately went to Dr. Taylor's office. When I arrived, I saw Logan sitting in front of her desk. Then, Dr. Taylor motioned me to come in, so I closed the door and sat down next to Logan.

"I just spoke with Michael regarding his emails resigning and then rescinding his resignation," I said. "When I asked him what was going on, he said to talk to you."

"I find it interesting that you couldn't bring yourself to call him when he resigned," she said, nastily, "but you found the time to call him when he rescinded his resignation."

"That's not true. I tried to call him multiple times after I received his first email, but apparently he was meeting with you--"

"*Yes, he was!*" She said in an angry tone. "*And I talked him out of resigning!*"

I sat there for a minute trying to process what was happening and noticing that Logan was being particularly quiet.

Then Dr. Taylor continued, "Ebony, I'm going to cut to the chase. You're being investigated for harassment, so I suggest you do some serious soul searching."

"*I'm being investigated for harassment?*" I asked. "I've never harassed a single person in my entire life!"

"You harassed Michael when you found out he met with Logan!" She yelled. "Logan said you humiliated Michael in front of him and threatened him, saying he would lose his job if he ever went above your head again! He resigned to get away from you!"

It was at that moment that I realized everything starting from the day Dr. Taylor stopped by my office to inform me about Michael's secret conversation with Logan was a ruse, and it broke my heart to discover that Logan was actively participating and conspiring with Dr. Taylor and Michael to assassinate my character and destroy my career.

"That's not true," I said, on the verge of crying as I turned to Logan. "You were there, Logan, why are you helping Dr. Taylor set me up?*"

Dr. Taylor leaned back in her chair, gave me a nasty smile, and calmly said, "Things can go from bad to worse in the blink of an eye. I suggest you leave before you say something you'll regret."

As I walked out of Dr. Taylor's office, I was panic stricken, and frantically trying to figure out what to do to save my job. When I arrived at my office, I closed the door, sunk into my chair, and cried, as a river of tears poured down my face.

If setting me up for harassment and firing me was her plan all along, why go through the trouble of promoting me and giving me such a large raise? I thought to myself. *Why not just fire me, and spare me the humiliation?*

No sooner had I asked the question than I already knew the answer. Dr. Taylor promoted me, and gave me the enormous raise, because she had no intention of paying it long-term. I was promoted at the beginning of March, and she was banking on firing me shortly thereafter.

On May 12, 2017, Steve Burger, the Corporate Director of Student Finance, who requested that I present at the Directors of Student Finance conference, sent the following email to all Chancellors, Vice Presidents of Finance, and Directors of Student Finance, announcing the Directors of Student Finance Conference dates and registration deadline:

From: Burger, Steve

Sent: Friday, May 12, 2017 8:57 AM

To: Chancellors; Dir of Student Finance; VPs of Finance

Cc: Burns, Aaron; Cockran, Esther; Markus, Mandy; Putnam, Donna; Scott, Melinda; Truscell, Dean

Subject: 2017 Directors of Student Finance Annual Conference

The Corporate Student Finance Team is proud to invite you to join us for a week of training, activities, and networking at the 2017 Directors of Student Finance Conference to be held at Corporate from June 19, 2017 through June 23, 2017. This conference is mandatory for student finance personnel and one SF leader from each campus is required to attend.

When I received the email announcing the Directors of Student Finance Conference, it was like pouring salt into an open wound. Steve Burger selected me to present at this conference, and that honor was taken away from me by Dr. Taylor and given to Michael. And since Corporate required at least one student finance leader from each campus to attend, and I was the only one at the Temple campus, I was required to attend the conference and receive training from Michael, my racist employee, during the break out session I was supposed to provide training in, and doing so would humiliate me beyond measure.

Before I had a chance to reach out to Logan and Dr. Taylor to inquire about registering for the conference, Logan forwarded Steve Burger's email directly to Dr. Taylor, and excluded me from the email string.

98

An hour later, Dr. Taylor responded to Logan's email, and mistakenly copied me on her response.

From: Taylor, Karen

Sent: Friday, May 12, 2017 11:37 AM

To: MacDougal, Logan

Cc: Ardoin, Ebony

Subject: RE: 2017 Directors of Student Finance Annual Conference

This is a laugh I needed today!

Hold off. If she asks, tell her I'm working on it and will let her know...

Karen

As painful as their emails were to read, I was glad Dr. Taylor made a Freudian slip when she accidently copied me on her response to Logan. Their email exchange was not only more evidence I could use to prove racial discrimination, but it also gave me insight into the date I would be fired. Logan suggested holding off on allowing me to register for the conference because the deadline wasn't until May 31st, which was two weeks away. And as I read between the lines, I knew that I would be fired within the next two weeks for the bogus harassment of Michael.

On May 22, 2017, I woke up panic stricken after another sleepless night, and terrified I would be fired when I arrived at work. So, after thanking God for waking me up in my right state of mind, and in my physically healthy body, at 6:30 a.m., I called Aaron Burns, the Chief Student Finance Officer at Corporate who was the one person I hoped I could count on for help. I assumed he wasn't in the office yet, and planned to leave an urgent voice message, but when he answered the phone, I immediately burst into tears, unable to control my emotions.

"I-I'm sorry to call you like this, Aaron," I said, crying my eyes out. "This is Ebony from the Daebrun Temple campus. I need your help."

"I'll help if I can," Aaron said. "What's going on?"

For the next thirty minutes, I explained to Aaron about the racial discrimination, racially hostile work environment, and race-based harassment I was enduring at the Temple campus. I informed him that immediately after Dr. Taylor became Chancellor, she began targeting me as the only Black person in a management position calling my braided hair worms, and saying things like "you don't sound black" in front of the other non-Black directors during management meetings. I also informed him that after Mom was diagnosed with stage four colon cancer, Dr. Taylor blocked my promotion to National Director, and ordered me to stop attending the SF Leadership Calls so my White employee could replace me. And on the same day, she ordered me to discontinue having any contact with him, or anyone else at Corporate.

Then, she started secretly meeting with my White employee every day behind closed doors for hours, forcing me to do his work, and mine, to keep the department running smoothly. And denied Steve Burger's request for my participation as a presenter at the upcoming Directors of Student Finance Conference, and gave that honor which was bestowed upon me to my White employee. I explained that Dr. Taylor, Logan, and Michael, conspired together to create a ruse, set me up under false pretenses, and have me unjustly investigated for harassment.

"Ebony, this is deeply disturbing," Aaron said.

"I'm trying to fight, but I'm emotionally bankrupt and completely exhausted," I said in between sniffles. "I can't, I can't function in this abusive environment any longer."

"I'll do what I can to help," Aaron replied. "You have one of the most positive attitudes I've ever seen, and I'm sorry this is happening to you."

After thanking Aaron for any help he could provide and hanging up, I documented the conversation in my Daily Log and then got dressed, and drove to work, praying the entire way.

"Father, please strap me in your armor," I said, "and form a hedge around me, and protect me from those people at Daebrun who are doing evil against me and doing me harm. In Jesus holy, mighty, and beautiful name I pray. Amen."

When I arrived at work, I fully expected to be harassed by Logan, abused by Dr. Taylor, accused by Michael, or fired on the spot. But when I walked through the front doors, the air on campus was noticeably different. Normally, the air was heavy, dark, and so thick it could choke a whale. But this time, the air seemed a little lighter, a little fresher. So, I took a deep breath in, let it out slowly, and proceeded to go to my office.

For the next four hours, Logan, Dr. Taylor, and Michael avoided me like I had a contagious disease. None of them interacted with me or bothered me, and I experienced a peace I hadn't felt in a long time. But at 1PM, when I arrived in the conference room for the weekly campus management meeting, I discovered where all the heavy, dark, and thick air went. It went to the conference room. When I walked in, every campus leader from Dr. Taylor on down was intensely staring at me, and if looks could kill, I would've been dead on arrival. The only one who wasn't staring me down was Christine Shaw, the Director of Enrollments, and my friend.

Shortly after the meeting was underway, things seemingly returned to normal. Dr. Taylor gave her opening remarks and review of agenda items as she always did, followed by departmental updates by each leader. It wasn't until the last ten minutes, during Dr. Taylor's closing remarks, that things went sideways.

"As a reminder, your risk assessment matrix is due to me no later than Wednesday," Dr. Taylor said. "And I would be remiss not to mention that Ebony complained to Corporate about campus level business, and is now approved to participate in the SF Leadership Calls. Congratulations, Ebony."

After being humiliated in the conference room, I couldn't get out of there fast enough. I was grateful to Aaron, though, for addressing one aspect of the discrimination I was dealing with so quickly, and hoped he had the power as the Chief Student Finance Officer at Corporate, to ensure that the remaining discriminatory acts committed by Dr. Taylor, Logan, and Michael would be dealt with equally as swiftly.

The next morning after I arrived at work, I received a phone call from Tiffany Mathers, the Corporate Director of Human Resources, and someone I had never personally met. She said she had spoken with Aaron Burns and wanted to get more information about the racial discrimination I disclosed to him.

After providing her with the same information I provided to Aaron during our phone conversation, I emailed her the supporting documentation I had been saving as evidence to prove my claims of racial discrimination, and she said she would review my documentation and get back with me. Then, I saved the email I sent as evidence that proved my employer was aware of the racial discrimination I was enduring. This was important because when I researched workplace harassment years ago after Ms. Kelly started harassing me, I read that your employer must be made aware of the racial discrimination you are being subjected to and given a reasonable amount of time to resolve the issues before you can file a formal discrimination complaint with either the federal or state civil rights agencies.

The atmosphere on campus for the remainder of the week was pretty much the same. Dr. Taylor, Logan, and Michael continued going to great lengths to avoid all contact with me, which made me quite happy. And at the end of the day on Friday, I left work and breathed a huge sigh of relief because I was officially on vacation so now they would have to wait until I returned if they wanted to fire me. Thank goodness I was smart enough to get my two-week vacation approved by Dr. Romano before she was fired and replaced by Dr. Taylor. And even though it wasn't the best time to be away from the office, with so many people conspiring against me, I felt like I was drowning, and needed to disconnect from work for my mental health and emotional well-being.

As I left for the day, I was convinced that by the time I returned from vacation, Corporate's investigation of my racial discrimination claims would be complete, the issues would be addressed head on thanks to Aaron Burn's involvement, and I would finally have an opportunity to work in an environment free of racism, hostility, and abuse...or so I thought.

CHAPTER 12

Thank God for Medical Leave

On June 5, 2017, I returned to work from my much-needed vacation, hopeful that Corporate had completed their investigation, and things had returned to normal. Sadly, my hopes were crushed when my employee, Marisol, rushed into my office, closed the door, and provided me with information that knocked me for a loop.

"Man, things were crazy-crazy while you were gone, boss!" She exclaimed, as she ran into my office, closed the door, and threw herself into the chair in front of my desk. "You know that, umm, VP of Finance from Oregon? I think her name is Meagan."

"Yeah, I've never met her, but I've heard of her," I replied.

"That bitch was here boss, asking 'bout everything we do."

"I didn't know she was coming here," I responded.

"Yeah, boss, I know! Michael was with her acting like he's my supervisor and I said man, you better get outta my face with that."

Then she said Logan, pulled her aside, and instructed her not to mention Meagan's visit to me if I called while I was on vacation. So, she waited until I returned to tell me what was going on.

After thanking her for having my back and assuring her I would not betray her trust, she returned to her cubicle, and I sat in my office completely stunned. I couldn't believe Logan brought the Vice President of Finance at the Portland, Oregon campus to Temple, to interrogate my staff while I was on vacation, and without my knowledge. And not only did Logan keep Meagan's visit a secret from me, but he also instructed

Marisol to keep her visit a secret from me, as well, undermining my position as the Senior Director of Student Finance, once again.

It was at that moment that I realized I was being retaliated against for reporting the racial discrimination I was enduring to Corporate, and Corporate didn't do a thing to protect me. They left me vulnerable to further discrimination as Logan, Michael, and Dr. Taylor moved full speed ahead with their plans to destroy my reputation, derail my career, and replace me with Michael.

The next day, upon my arrival at work, I immediately received a call from Logan summoning me to his office. Logan never called me to his office for anything, he always came to mine because he prided himself on getting in ten thousand steps a day, and the walk down three flights of stairs, and then to my office, helped him get closer to achieving his daily step goal. So, when he summoned me to his office, my radar instantly went up and I was alarmed. And when I arrived and saw Michael, I knew in no uncertain terms, that the anxiety I felt was warranted.

Oh no! I thought to myself as I walked in, closed the door behind me, and sat down next to Michael in front of Logan's desk.

"While you were gone," Logan said, examining me with the coldest of eyes as Michael watched, "several issues came to the surface exposing gaps in many of the processes you developed."

"What issues and what gaps?" I asked.

Logan ignored my question and instead began asking me question after question about the processes we use to package students, manage the default rate, request federal funds, and so on, and for each question, I had a valid answer. But it was obvious that Logan wasn't interested in my answers because he continued badgering me in the presence of Michael, questioning the accuracy of the processes I developed, and throwing shade at me.

"I'm no expert," he said. "But it's clear there are gaps in your processes that need to be address."

Frustrated, I said, "Our campus successfully passed *the federal audit with zero findings* based on the strength of my processes. And if the federal auditors couldn't find anything wrong, and the Chief Student Finance Officer at Corporate couldn't find anything wrong, and the processes I developed were so strong that Corporate asked me to train seventy campuses on the Leadership Call *and* at the Directors of

Student Finance Conference, I don't understand how you, someone with no SF experience at all, found gaps."

"Because there are gaps!" Michael yelled, turning his head to me so fast he gave himself whiplash. "And that's why I'm coming up with better processes that don't leave room for error!"

Suddenly, the light bulb turned on, and I now understood why Logan was so eager to obtain my process documentation back in April. He had no intention of using it as a guide to train other department heads on how to document and flow chart their processes. He wanted to give my documentation to Michael, so he could attempt to dissect it, try moving a few things around, add a few things here or remove a few things there, and then take credit for developing "better processes".

Ignoring Michael, I continued looking at Logan. "If you have concerns with my performance, I'd appreciate you meeting with me in private, not in the presence of my employee."

"You're right," Logan said, displaying no signs of regret. "I'll send you a calendar invite."

As I walked out of his office, I knew I was still in danger of being fired, but I also knew I was being retaliated against for complaining to Corporate about the racism I was enduring. And now, firing me wasn't good enough anymore. Now, Dr. Taylor was on a mission to assassinate my character, and ruin my reputation to such a degree that I would be labeled by all as incompetent, and unable to seek gainful employment as a Senior Director or otherwise at any of the other sixty-nine Corporate owned campuses.

The humiliation I suffered during the meeting with Logan and Michael was the straw that broke the camel's back. So, when I returned to my office, I closed the door and placed a frantic call to Tiffany Mathers, the Corporate Director of Human Resources, that I spoke with in May. When she answered, I broke down and cried, as I explained the details of the humiliating meeting that had just taken place, a meeting that I believed was an act of retaliation for reporting the discrimination I was enduring to both her and Aaron Burns in May.

"I trusted you," I frustratingly said, through sniffles. "And your lack of action gave them the opportunity to retaliate against me."

"I promise you," Tiffany said. "I'm looking into this and will get back with you soon."

Great, more empty promises, I thought to myself.

After the discouraging conversation I had with Tiffany, I decided that enough was enough because I had done everything in my power to coexist with the racists at the Temple campus and things were not improving, they were getting worse. It was at this point that I decided it was time to send the written discrimination complaint, via email, that I had been preparing for since the day Dr. Taylor arrived. The discrimination complaint containing ironclad evidence of racial discrimination, similar to the one I submitted against Malcolm Webb years ago that resulted in his termination, but stronger because of years of documentation I had collected.

Initially, my plan was to spend the rest of my day preparing my discrimination complaint but Marisol, my loyal employee, was bombarded with students and was drowning because Michael was missing in action, as usual. And since I couldn't bear the thought of letting her drown, especially after the kindness and support she faithfully showed me, I chose to help Marisol, and spent my entire day meeting with what seemed like an endless line of students, while also stressing about how much longer I would have my job.

When I made it home after a long day of work, I was completely wiped out. So, I made my son dinner, climbed into bed, and took comfort in knowing that I would have an opportunity to draft my discrimination complaint, and send the email after mom's chemo appointment in the morning.

The following day, I worked remotely and took Mom to her chemo appointment. It was wonderful spending time with Mom in chemo even though it was under such dire circumstances.

"Are things gettin' any better at work, honey?" Mom asked, leaning back in her recliner chair as the nurse draped a heated blanket over her.

"No, mom, things are a lot worse," I responded. "But don't worry, I'm fighting back. After chemo is done, I'm going to file a formal discrimination complaint."

"That's my girl," Mom said, with tired eyes and a faint smile.

Although Mom was weak from months of chemo treatments, we made the most of our time together by watching mom's favorite show about aspiring models trying to catch their big break in the fashion industry, and making bets about which models would be eliminated.

Spending time with Mom was a wonderful distraction, and for a few shining hours I forgot about the horrors awaiting me at work the next day. That is, until I received a phone call from my friend, Christine Shaw, the Director of Enrollments. Christine respected my time away from the office, and rarely called because she knew I was with mom. So, when I received her call, I knew it was important and answered it.

"Can you talk? She asked. "We really need to talk."

I could tell by the tone in her voice that something was seriously wrong, and it gave me a sick feeling in the pit of my stomach.

"I'm with my Mom in chemo. Give me a few minutes to find a quiet place, and I'll call you right back," I replied, trying not to alert Mom to the fact that something was wrong.

After hanging up, I told Mom I was stepping out for a few minutes to make a call. I also notified a member of the clinic staff that I was stepping out, and to call me on my cell if they needed to reach me.

When I was in my car, I called Christine back.

"What's going on?" I asked.

"The shit hit the fan today and I'm resigning," she replied.

"Oh no! What happened?"

Christine explained that after she was hired, things were great for the first four months, because Dr. Taylor didn't realize she was Black.

"She assumed I was White. Always commenting on my pretty blue eyes and tanned skin," Christine said. "And I wasn't about to correct her because I saw how she was always mean mugging you, no offense."

"None taken," I replied. "I get it. But why are you resigning?"

Christine said everything changed two months ago, when Dr. Taylor stopped by her office and noticed the family photo of Christine, her Black husband, and their two Black children sitting on her desk. She said Dr. Taylor didn't say anything, but she's been harassing and denigrating her ever since.

"When you were on vacation, Ebony, she brought a box of king size chocolate bars to the campus management meeting, and told everyone to help themselves. So, everyone did. But when I opened the wrapper, and put the chocolate in my mouth, before I bit it, she started snickering and said, 'I knew you'd like having a big, chocolate bar in your mouth,' and I knew exactly what she meant, and so did everyone else by the look on their faces."

Then Christine said she started demeaning her in front of her staff and sending her hostile emails that undermined her position as the Director of Enrollments. And when she complained to Travis Clayton, the National Director of Human Resources at the Austin campus, nothing was done, and instead she was retaliated against by Dr. Taylor. She said Dr. Taylor cornered her in her office behind closed doors, and threatened her, saying that going to H.R. wasn't going to work. She also warned her that things could go from bad to worse quick. And as I listened to Christine, I could hear the hurt in her voice, as an all too familiar feeling came over me.

"Life's too short to put up with this shit," she said. "That's why I'm resigning."

"I'm so sorry, Christine," I said, with tears in my eyes. "I had no idea. But if it makes you feel any better, Dr. Taylor's been discriminating against me, too."

"I know," she replied. "Which brings me to the other reason I called. I couldn't leave without telling you that when you return to work tomorrow, they're going to fire you."

"Oh my God! Are you sure?" I exclaimed.

"I'm sure. They've been conspiring against you for months."

"Who?"

"Dr. Taylor, Logan and Michael. Every Wednesday when you're gone, they meet in your office and go through your things. I got concerned and started watching them last week. I don't have any proof, but my gut tells me they're setting you up for forgery, or making it look like you falsified records."

"But how do you know I'm getting fired tomorrow?"

Christine then said that Travis Clayton, the National Director of Human Resources in Austin, was at the Temple campus as we were speaking interviewing Michael and Marisol, and meeting with Dr. Taylor, Logan, and Michael behind closed doors. She said the buzz around campus was that I was going to be fired when I returned to work in the morning, and Travis was staying in a hotel overnight so he'd arrive on campus first thing in the morning, and catch me when I arrived.

After thanking Christine for giving me the heads up, I hung up the phone and sat in my car, staring out the window and trying to figure out what to do to keep from getting fired when I returned to work.

Suddenly, I was overcome by intense fear, and couldn't catch my breath. My heart was racing a million miles a minute as a crippling sensation moved from my head to deep in my chest.

"God, please help me," I cried out before swinging the car door open and vomiting on the ground below.

Mom was still in chemotherapy, but I was in my car on the verge of some kind of mental or nervous breakdown. So, I called my sister Gabrielle in a panic, hysterically explained what was happening, and when she arrived at the clinic to stay with mom, I drove myself as fast as I could to my primary care doctor, instead of the emergency room, because I was closer to him.

By the time I made it to the check-in desk, I was hyperventilating and crying hysterically as everyone in the lobby stared at me and watched.

"Are you okay?" The woman manning the check-in desk asked. "Do you have an appointment?"

"H-Help me, please," I said as I gasped for air. "I-I need to see my doctor."

The woman at the reception desk was kind, and after collecting my driver's license and insurance card, she checked me in even though I didn't have an appointment.

It didn't take long for a nurse to come out, call my name, and escort me to the back area to weigh me, take my blood pressure, and ask several questions related to my medical history. As I did my best to answer each question, tear after tear rolled down my cheeks. Then, I followed her to an exam room, and waited for the doctor.

When the doctor finally arrived, he read the notes from my chart, and said, "Your blood pressure is high. What's going on?"

As soon as he asked that question, I broke into hysterical crying again and started rambling. "I- I feel like I'm losing my mind. I'm so stressed my hair's falling out. I'm crying all the time. I don't think I can handle much more. I've been having chest pains. I'm depressed, I'm terrified, I can barely function, I've gained eighty pounds in less than a year, I'm drowning--"

"What's causing this enormous amount of stress?" The doctor asked, calmly interrupting me.

"Are you listening to me!" I screamed, interrupting the doctor as I cried hysterically. "I have shortness of breath. I can hardly move around because I've gained so much weight. I can barely sleep but when I do sleep, I have nightmares. I'm scared all the time. I'm worried all the

time. I'm exhausted, I think about suicide sometimes, my hair is falling out--"

"Take a deep breath Ms. Ardoin," the doctor said, "And try to calmly tell me what's causing you to be in distress."

After taking a few deep breaths and letting them out slowly, I said, in between sniffles, "My Mom has stage four colon cancer, and I'm afraid for her, so very afraid. I can't bear the thought of losing mom, and I'm doing everything I can to help, but to make matter's worse, at work I've been the target of vicious racism, and so in addition to taking care of my Mom and my son, I've been working seventy to eighty hours each week trying to keep up with my workload, and documenting the racial discrimination I've been enduring to protect myself."

"How long have you been under this level of stress?"

"For about five years."

The doctor handed me a box of tissues, and as I began to dry my eyes, he placed his stethoscope on my back and told me to breathe deeply a couple of times. Afterwards, he placed it above my chest and had me inhale and exhale.

"I believe you're suffering from recurring panic attacks, severe anxiety, and major depression caused by stress," he said.

Then, he gave me a prescription for an anti-depressant containing anti-anxiety elements, and put me on a medical leave of absence from work for one week, from June 7th through June 14th.

After leaving the doctor's office, I immediately emailed the medical leave documentation to Dr. Taylor, Logan, Travis Clayton, the National Director of Human Resources, and Tiffany Mathers, the Corporate Director of Human Resources. And since they couldn't fire me while I was on an approved medical leave of absence, my job was protected for at least the next seven days.

Still, I'm sure Dr. Taylor was confident her plan to fire me would go off without a hitch when I returned from my medical leave a week later, and she could proceed with replacing me with Michael and live happily ever after...or so *she* thought.

CHAPTER 13

The Squeaky Wheel Gets the Grease

When I got home from the doctor, I called Gabrielle to make sure everything went ok with mom. Then, I took the email documentation I had been collecting since the day Dr. Taylor was hired, put the evidence in chronological order by date, and renamed each piece of evidence Attachment 1, Attachment 2, Attachment 3, and so on. Then, using the information contained in my Daily Log to jog my memory of everything that happened over the last five years, I drafted my formal discrimination complaint email containing ironclad proof of racial discrimination. Because I had so much evidence, it took me almost seven hours to draft the email. And since I trusted absolutely no one at the campus level, the national level, or the corporate level, this time, I was going to jump over everyone's head, and email my complaint directly to the CEO at Corporate. And because I didn't trust her either, and there was no one else in a higher position at Corporate, I did some research and obtained the names and email addresses of three people on the Board of Directors and I was going to copy them on my email, as well as Aaron Burns, the Chief Student Finance Officer at Corporate who tried to help me, and Tiffany Mathers, the National Director of Human Resources whose lack of action resulted in additional retaliation.

With so many people in the know, there was no way anyone could ignore my complaint. And even if they tried to, I was okay with that, because I had collected enough evidence proving systemic racism and racial discrimination in my workplace, and was ready to file a formal

Racial Discrimination Complaint with the State of Texas Workforce Commission Civil Rights Division and retain an attorney, if necessary.

The email I drafted was seventeen pages long, and contained fifty-nine pages of evidence in the form of emails from Dr. Taylor, emails from Logan MacDougal, emails pertaining to my outstanding performance, pictures of awards I received, my outstanding performance review, before and after audit reports, emails I had sent to various people, and my Daily Log which provided a detailed, chronological description of every discriminatory conversation and discriminatory event that had occurred while I was employed at the Temple campus.

At 9:02PM, I emailed the following discrimination complaint to Charlotte Brice, the CEO at Corporate:

From: Ardoin, Ebony

Sent: Wednesday, June 07, 2017 9:02 PM

To: Brice, Charlotte

Cc: Burns, Aaron; Mathers, Tiffany; Montgomery, Avis; Rory, Luke; Klinger, Nancy

Subject: Racial Discrimination, Race-Based Harassment and Racially Hostile Work Environment

Dear Ms. Brice,

My name is Ebony Ardoin, and I am a Black employee who was originally hired at Daebrun Career Institute in January 2012 as the Senior Secretary at the Austin campus. In April 2013, I was demoted to Student Finance Advisor at the Austin campus, and in July 2015, I was promoted to Director of Student Finance at the Temple campus, where I was the only Black employee in a management position until November 2016. In March 2017, I was promoted to Senior Director of Student Finance at the Temple campus, and this is the position I currently hold.

Although my career at Daebrun has progressed over the years, I continue to have problems with campus-level supervisors, executives in the Daebrun system, and coworkers which have been the result of both veiled and blatant racial discrimination. The most recent incident occurred today. Furthermore, the Chancellor at the Temple campus has communicated her racist preferences to my White employee, as well as my direct supervisor and others, creating a racially hostile work environment for me.

I am sending this email to you, along with supporting attachments, in an attempt to internally resolve my discrimination issues in lieu of filing a formal Racial Discrimination

112

Complaint with the Texas Workforce Commission Civil Rights Division and retaining an attorney. My complaint, which documents the racial discrimination, racially hostile work environment, racially based preferential treatment of my White employee, and retaliation, is based on the following:

Then, over the next seventeen pages of the email, I provided a factual breakdown, in chronological order, of every discriminatory event that had occurred starting from the day I was hired as the Senior Secretary at the Austin campus. The breakdown included the discriminatory acts committed by Ms. Kelly in 2012, 2013, and 2014, continued with the discriminatory acts committed by Malcolm Webb and Ms. Kelly in 2015, listed the discriminatory acts committed by Kyle Charron in 2016, and finished with the back-to-back discriminatory acts committed by Dr. Taylor, Logan MacDougal, and Michael Sullivan in 2016 and 2017. For each discriminatory act that I listed in the email, I included the number of the Attachment(s) that proved, beyond a shadow of a doubt, that what I was saying was true.

The email ended with the following information:

The racial discrimination, racially hostile work environment, racially based preferential treatment of my White employee, retaliation, failure to promote me to National Director of Student Finance, and Daebrun's failure to properly address the issues detailed in this and previous discrimination complaints in accordance with Texas state law, as well as its own no discrimination and harassment policies, has caused me severe and extreme anguish, panic attacks, physical and emotional exhaustion, anxiety, depression, humiliation, anger, nervousness, sleeplessness, embarrassment, fear, and severe emotional distress.

I am currently on a medical leave of absence, expected to return back to work on June 14, 2017, and am terrified to return to a campus where unrelenting harassment, discrimination, and retaliation are the theme of the day. And since I previously reported the discrimination I was enduring to Tiffany Mathers, the Corporate Director of Human Resources, on May 23rd, and suffered retaliation due to her lack of action, I have lost all confidence in Corporate's ability to protect me, or prevent further discrimination and harassment upon my return to work.

As I previously mentioned, at this time I have not filed a formal Racial Discrimination Complaint with the Texas Workforce Commission Civil Rights Division nor retained an attorney because I am hopeful we can come to a resolution internally that satisfies both parties and makes me whole.

Thank you for listening and I look forward to hearing from you.

After sending the email, I checked on my son who was watching TV in the family room, melted into the mattress, and fell fast asleep from pure emotional exhaustion.

On the morning of June 13th, the day before I was scheduled to return to work from my medical leave, I received a phone call on my cell. When I realized the caller was Logan, I was overcome by a feeling of nervousness that was so powerful, it caused my hands to tremble. Unable to handle a phone conversation with Logan, I intentionally ignored the call, and when I didn't answer, he left me a voice message.

"Hi Ebony, this is Logan," he said. "Just trying to touch base and let you know that we miss you, and are looking forward to your return tomorrow. Give me a call when you have a chance. Thanks."

When I listened to Logan's message, I became upset, because I knew the reason they were looking forward to my return was to fire my ass.

That afternoon, I drove to my doctor's office for my one-week follow-up visit and by the time I got there, I was falling apart at the seams. After explaining what happened when I received Logan's phone call, the doctor determined that Logan was one of several triggers causing my anxiety and panic attacks. And because I was in no condition mentally or emotionally to talk to Logan let alone see him, my doctor extended my medical leave for an additional two weeks through June 28th. And since they couldn't fire me while I was on an approved medical leave, my job was protected for at least the next fourteen days.

After I left my doctor's office, I immediately emailed the medical leave documentation to Logan, Dr. Taylor, Travis Clayton, the National Director of Human Resources, and Tiffany Mathers, the Corporate Director of Human Resources.

Ten minutes later, I received three back-to-back calls from Logan that I intentionally ignored, and when I listened to the voice message he left, I could hear the anxiety in his voice, and knew they were finding it more difficult to do my job than they anticipated.

"Ebony, I hope you come back soon," he desperately said. "SF is falling apart, and we could really use your help. Please call me."

When I listened to Logan's message, I laughed for the first time in weeks.

"Just use the *better processes* Michael came up with," I said out loud, amusing myself.

114

As I reflected back on the whirlwind of events that occurred during the month of June, I was amazed at how God used Christine Shaw, my dear friend at the Temple campus, to provide me with the information about being fired, that caused my mental breakdown, which resulted in my medical leave of absence, that stopped me from returning to work, which prevented me from being fired, and gave me the time I needed to submit my formal, written discrimination complaint to the CEO at Corporate, and finally get the upper hand in my fight against systemic racism at Daebrun.

The next day, I received a call from Tiffany Mathers, the Corporate Director of Human Resources, and this time I answered the call.

"I just saw your email. Your medical leave was extended again?"

"Yes."

"The VP of Finance in Temple is really freaking out. He said things are a disaster there and he doesn't know what to do."

"Really? How so?" I calmly asked, using the same words that Logan once used against me when I told him Michael was behaving inappropriately.

"Apparently, something went wrong when your employee, Michael, tried to request federal funds. The funds weren't received, and they missed the deadline for issuing stipend checks to hundreds of angry students."

Missing the deadline to issue stipend checks was a *very big deal* because many of the students who borrowed extra student loan funds needed their stipend check to pay their rent or mortgage payments. I've seen the wrath of students who do not receive their stipend checks on time, and it's a scary predicament to be in. But did I feel sorry for Michael after he screwed things up? I did not.

"Many of them have already contacted the Department of Ed or have threatened to withdraw," she said. "Logan was hoping to get some guidance from you on how to resolve the issue, but said you refuse to answer any of his calls. Is this correct?"

"Yes," I replied. "Logan is one of the triggers causing my medical issues. My doctor has instructed me not to have verbal or physical contact with him while I'm on medical leave."

Tiffany said she understood and went on to say that because I didn't have any vacation days left, she would email me the paperwork to apply for the Family and Medical Leave Act (FMLA), as well as short-term disability, not Worker's Compensation, because the medical conditions diagnosed by my doctor were caused by a combination of stress at work and at home. Not all companies offer short-term disability to their employees, so I was glad I worked for an employer who offered it.

Shortly after hanging up, I received the email from Tiffany and learned that FMLA, according to the U.S. Department of Labor's Wage and Hour Division, entitled me to take up to twelve workweeks of unpaid, job-protected leave in a twelve-month period for the serious health conditions diagnosed by my doctor, which were preventing me from performing my job. And short-term disability, according to the forms Tiffany emailed me, would pay me up to sixty-six percent of the compensation I was earning before my disability occurred for up to one hundred fifty days during any twelve-month period.

Knowing that Dr. Taylor couldn't fire me for up to twelve weeks because FMLA would protect my job, *and* that short-term disability would pay me a large portion of my salary while I was on medical leave, gave me a huge sense of relief. So, I immediately completed both applications and emailed them back to Tiffany the same day. Twenty-four hours later, I was approved for FMLA and three weeks later, I was approved for short-term disability.

Fourteen days had passed since the day I emailed my racial discrimination complaint and supporting evidence to the CEO at Corporate, and I had not received a single response from her, or anyone else who was copied on the email. So, to let them know how serious I was about getting justice for myself, I moved forward with filing my Racial Discrimination Complaint with the Texas Workforce Commission Civil Rights Division. Afterwards, I emailed a copy to the CEO at Corporate, and copied everyone else who was included on the previous email I had sent. Again, I did not receive a single response.

On June 27, 2017, one day before I was scheduled to return to work from my medical leave, I met with my doctor again for my follow-up appointment, provided him with a copy of the discrimination complaint I emailed to the CEO weeks ago, and informed him that I had not received a response from anyone, and was terrified that nothing had changed and the racially hostile work environment was still there. So, he extended my medical leave again for four more weeks, and when I emailed my medical documentation to Logan, Dr. Taylor, and Travis Clayton, the National Human Resources Director, I got the feeling that this was the moment when they realized they had bit off more than they could chew with thinking that firing me was going to be easy. Mom always said the squeaky wheel gets the grease, and with the extended medical leave I was on causing my department to fall apart, the email I sent to the CEO and Board of Directors shining a bright spot light on the racial discrimination occurring at the Temple campus, and the Racial Discrimination Complaint that I filed with the Texas Workforce Commission Civil Rights Division bringing the state government into the loop, *all four wheels* on my career bus were squeaking louder than worn out car brakes as I fought back, with everything in my power, against systemic racism in my workplace.

One month had passed since the day I sent my racial discrimination complaint email to the CEO at Corporate, and I still had not received a single response from her, or anyone else copied on the email. I also had not received a single response from anyone to the email I sent notifying them that I had filed a Racial Discrimination Complaint with the State of Texas.

Concerned my emails weren't being delivered, I placed a call to Tiffany Mathers, the Corporate Director of Human Resources, to follow up and discovered, to my surprise, that she had resigned or been fired two days after I emailed the CEO at Corporate notifying her that I had filed a Racial Discrimination Complaint with the State of Texas.

To ensure that Dr. Taylor, Logan, and Michael knew that I had emailed my racial discrimination complaint against them to the CEO at Corporate, and filed a Racial Discrimination Complaint against them with the State of Texas, I forwarded both emails to Dr. Taylor, Logan, and Travis Clayton, the National Human Resources Director. My emails must've put fear in their hearts because two days later, my access to my company email account was revoked, in an attempt to prevent me from gathering evidence I could use against them, as well as my access to the company Intranet which contained their policy data and employee handbook. But little did they know, I already had smoking gun evidence that proved my claims of racial discrimination because I had been diligently collecting hard evidence against them for about six months.

The next day, I went on the hunt for an attorney to represent me against Daebrun, and it didn't take long before I sparked the interest of a female attorney in Austin, Texas, who specialized in employment law and litigation and had over twenty years of experience. When I spoke with her over the phone, explained what was happening to me, and told her that I had a complete timeline of every racial discrimination event that had occurred (my Daily Log) as well as fifty-nine pages of supporting evidence, she waived her three-hundred-dollar consultation fee, scheduled an appointment to meet with me, and took me on as a client that very day. Now that I had retained an attorney and filed my discrimination complaint with the State of Texas, I was feeling better about my chances of surviving this horrible ordeal when I returned to work from my medical leave.

Still, Dr. Taylor was very cocky. And I'm sure she believed she could downplay the severity of the racial discrimination I reported, get a slap on the wrist from Corporate for using poor judgment, and still achieve her ultimate goal of firing me and replacing me with Michael...or so *she* thought.

CHAPTER 14

The Investigation Begins

The following week, my ghetto fabulous friend at the Austin campus, Latoya Johnson, invited me to lunch. We met at an Italian restaurant, and after giving her the biggest hug, we sat down at the table, ordered our food, and started catching up.

"Remember how Malcolm used to discriminate against us?" I asked.

"Girl, who could forget," Latoya replied. "He was a nightmare."

"Well, his discrimination was a walk in the park compared to what I'm dealing with now," I said, as tears formed in my eyes.

Then, for the next thirty or so minutes, I poured my heart out to Latoya about everything I was struggling with concerning mom's cancer diagnosis, the discrimination at the Temple campus, and the reason I was on medical leave.

"I'm so sorry, girl," she said, with compassion in her eyes. "We just can't catch a break, can we?"

"We?" I asked. "You're having issues, too?"

"Yeah, things are really bad," she replied. "My husband said I should just quit. But I have a daughter now, I can't just up and quit."

Then, before I knew it, my dear friend broke down and I saw her cry for the very first time.

"Remember when they promoted me to Associate Director and gave me that funky thirty-five-thousand-dollar salary?" She asked.

"Yeah, that was insulting."

Then she said that after Kyle Charron was fired, Amanda Ross, the Chancellor at the Austin campus, assigned all of Kyle's National Director of Student Finance duties *for all campuses* to Latoya, and told her that the extra duties were temporary because I was being promoted to Kyle's position. But when my promotion to National Director fell through, Amanda didn't remove Kyle's duties from her plate. She forced her to continue doing the National Director duties, in addition to her own Associate Director duties.

"Did they increase your salary when they gave you Kyle's duties?" I asked. "You know he was making about eighty thousand a year."

"No, girl. I'm doing my job *and* Kyle's job, for thirty-five thousand dollars," she said, with tears pouring down her face. "I'm tired. I'm working ninety hours a week, I have a toddler at home, and a husband I never get to see, and I haven't been able to take any vacation time in over a year."

Latoya continued crying, and said that when she complained to Amanda Ross again about increasing her salary, and removing the National Director duties from her plate, Amanda increased her salary to a measly forty-four thousand dollars a year *to do both jobs*, and told her that instead of complaining she should be happy that she was gaining the type of experience that only comes once in a lifetime.

"Toy, they're discriminating against you. They're making you do a lot more work for a lot less pay because you're Black," I said. "Think about it. If Malcolm was making fifty-five thousand dollars a year, and Kyle was making let say eighty-thousand dollars, their two salaries combined equal one hundred and thirty-five thousand dollars a year. By forcing you to do both jobs for forty-four thousand, they're saving ninety-one thousand dollars a year by using you for slave labor."

"I know," she said with a sigh. "I think I'm gonna take my husband's advice and just quit."

After giving Latoya a hug, I informed her that I had retained an attorney to represent me against Daebrun, provided her with my attorney's contact information, and suggested she give her a call immediately and to let her know that I referred her.

After Latoya left, I reached out to my dear friend, Christine Shaw, the one who gave me the heads up that I was going to be fired before she quit due to racial discrimination, and provided her with my attorney's contact information, too.

A week later, my attorney informed me that she had taken both Latoya and Christine on as clients and shared with me that even though their individual cases were not as strong as mine because neither one had much tangible evidence, I had a very strong case and since all three of us worked for the same employer, my case added strength to their individual cases.

On July 26, 2017, I returned to work from my medical leave of absence and was shocked by how dirty and unorganized my office was, and how many stacks of documents, forms, and unopened mail were everywhere. As I sat down to begin my day, Michael walked in.

"Welcome back, Ebony!" He said, with a smile so wide I could see his wisdom teeth. "I'm so glad you're back!"

"It's good to be back," I replied, lying through my teeth.

Because my office looked like a disaster area, Marisol, my feisty and trusted employee, offered to help me get it cleaned and reorganized.

"OMG boss, I'm so glad your back!" She exclaimed as we vacuumed, dusted, and sorted through the smaller piles.

When the smaller piles were dissolved, Marisol started to grab the large pile of documents sitting on my tall file cabinet, but it was piled so high that the whole thing begin to fall over. Marisol quickly reacted to catch the falling documents, but she accidently caused my oak book clock containing a photo of my son to fall to the ground. When she picked it up, she was less concerned about the cracked glass and more concerned with something else.

"Ay, Dios mio!" She exclaimed, holding my book clock in her hands, and looking at me with the saddest of eyes.

"What's wrong, Mari?" I asked.

She didn't say a word. She just walked over to me and slowly handed me my book clock. "I'm so sorry, boss," she solemnly said.

When I flipped my book clock over, I was stunned as I realized what had upset Marisol. Apparently, while I was on medical leave, someone carved the word "NIGGER" on the back of my book clock in deep, dark, large letters. As I sat at my desk staring at the word and running my finger along the letters, my heart sank, and I don't think I could've felt any lower.

Then, I asked Marisol to give me a few moments alone and before she left, she gave me a warm hug.

After closing my eyes and taking a few deep breaths, I knew what I needed to do. So, I pulled out my smart phone, took pictures of my book clock from various angles, and attached the photos to the following email that I sent to the CEO at Corporate and Travis Clayton, the National Director of Human Resources:

From: Ardoin, Ebony
Sent: Wednesday, July 26, 2017 10:44 AM
To: Brice, Charlotte
Cc: Clayton, Travis
Subject: Racially Hostile Work Environment

Ms. Brice,

I returned from medical leave today, and while reorganizing my office with the help of my employee, Marisol Gutierrez, she discovered that the word "NIGGER" had been carved into the back of my oak book clock in deep, dark, large letters when it fell to the ground after she reacted to a pile of documents falling from the top of my filing cabinet.

Words cannot express how angry this makes me! This is my first day back and this is what I return to?

Ebony Ardoin, Senior Director of Student Finance

After sending the email, I forwarded a copy to my attorney, and continued working, trying not to let what happened eat at me. And although I never received a response to my email, things went relatively well for the rest of the week as Dr. Taylor and Logan avoided me like I was a skunk.

The following week, a team of investigators sent by Corporate arrived at the Temple campus and everyone was on edge. When I saw them standing in the lobby, I assumed they were there to investigate the defacement of my book clock with the racial slur. But over the next four days, as the investigators interviewed me, my staff, all campus management leaders, including Dr. Taylor, and many others, it became clear that the investigators were there to do far more than just investigate my book clock incident. They were also gathering information about the racial discrimination I reported in the discrimination complaints I emailed to the CEO at Corporate and filed with the State of Texas. And as each day passed, the tension on campus continued to rise and it was obvious that Dr. Taylor, Logan, and Michael were worried about Corporate's involvement.

When the investigators left at the end of the week, Dr. Harry Gershon, the CEO for the Daebrun division, sent an email to all staff at the Temple campus reminding everyone about the policy prohibiting discrimination or harassment on the basis of race or any other protected class. The email also stated that anyone who was found to have engaged in such behavior, regardless of their title, would be subjected to corrective action, up to and including termination of employment.

When I read the email from the CEO, I knew the investigators found something that corroborated the racial discrimination I reported. Why else would Daebrun's CEO send such a strongly worded email denouncing discrimination and harassment on the basis of race? And even though I didn't know the extent of what they found, the email from Daebrun's CEO gave me a feeling of hope and ended my second week back at work on a high note.

But just as the CEO's email gave me hope, I'm certain it elicited a different kind of feeling in Dr. Taylor, Logan, and Michael, as the window they once had to hide the systemic racism at the Temple campus closed.

When I returned to work the following week, I felt like I had entered the twilight zone. Everyone on campus was walking on eggshells around me, being over-the-top sugary sweet, and bending over backwards to accommodate me. In fact, I received a visit from Logan, after he avoided me for two weeks straight, that was downright bizarre.

"Ebony, we were lost without you," he said, looking at me like a grinning idiot.

"Really? How so?" I asked, putting him on the spot.

There was an awkward silence in the room as he stared at me, still grinning, and I stared back at him.

"Well, your department was on its last legs, but now that your back, we'll be on top again in no time!"

"Thanks."

"No, thank you," he said, still grinning.

"Okay, well thanks for stopping by."

After Logan left, I continued to work, and the day went smoothly. I didn't have a single issue with anyone or anything.

I was planning to leave work at 4 p.m. to get a head start on the highway, but decided to work late because my team had fallen behind in completing financial aid packages while I was on medical leave, and I wanted to put a dent in the backlog. At 5 p.m., Marisol poked her head into my office, said adios, and left for the day. And Michael, who was working until 8 p.m. that night, remained in his cubicle and continued working.

At 7:30 p.m., I was worn out and decided to call it a day. So, I turned off the lights in my office, closed my door, and said goodnight to Michael as I walked past his cubicle and exited through the front door of the Student Finance department. Then, I walked down the long hallway, passed the back door of the Student Finance department which was always locked, and went to the ladies' room.

As I walked up the long hallway to leave, I realized I had left my green tea on my desk, and since I was closer to the back door of the Student Finance department, I unlocked it with my key and entered. But as I got closer to my office, I overheard Michael in his cubicle having a disturbing phone conversation about me with a coworker who apparently worked in the Enrollments department.

"I can't fucking stand Ebony!" He exclaimed! "I heard her meeting with your student today. She talked to him like he was two fucking years old! Dr. Taylor keeps telling me things will get better, that they're going to deal with her, but nothing's been done. They were supposed to fire her, but they let her ass come back!"

I wanted to secretly record Michael's phone conversation with my smart phone, but I knew it was against the law in Texas to record a conversation that I was not a party to. So, I continued listening as Michael referred to me using every expletive known to man, and knew I needed a witness, if I was going to prove that what I heard was true. So, I quietly exited the same way I had entered, found a coworker who was also working the late shift sitting in her office in the Career Services department, and briefly explained what was happening. Then, I asked her to follow me and listen to what was being said because I needed a witness, and she was more than willing to help.

As we quietly entered the back door to the Student Finance department and got closer to Michael's cubicle, he was still on the phone ranting about me.

"Fuck that Black bitch! I can't stand her ass! She should've been fired by now! I can't believe she's making us work overtime!"

As Michael continued describing me in the vilest of terms, the coworker I was with gave me a gentle nudge and whispered, "Come on, stop listening to him. It's not worth it."

After we left the area and returned to her office, I asked if I could use her computer to send an email to HR because I was too upset to return to my office. She agreed, so I sent the following email to Travis Clayton (the National Human Resources Director) and copied Dr. Taylor, Logan, and the CEO at Corporate:

From: Snowton, Debbie
Sent: Monday, July 31, 2017 8:06 PM
To: Clayton, Travis
Cc: Taylor, Karen; MacDougal, Logan; Brice, Charlotte
Subject: This is Ebony Ardoin Writing to You from Debbie Snowton's Computer

I am writing from Debbie's computer because I am too upset to return to my office. At 7:30 p.m., as I prepared to leave for the day, I turned off the lights in my office, closed my door, and said goodnight to Michael as I walked out. Then, I went to the ladies' room before beginning my commute and was about to leave when I realized I had left my green tea in my office. Because I was closer to the back door of the Student Finance department, I unlocked it with my key and entered.

As I got closer to my office, I heard Michael having a very disturbing phone conversation in his cubicle about me with a coworker saying, "I can't f*cking stand Ebony! I heard her meeting with your student today. She talked to him like he was two f*cking years old. I can't take it anymore! Dr. Taylor keeps telling me that things will get better, that they're going to deal with her, but nothing's been done! They were supposed to fire her, but they let her ass come back!"

Horrified, I continued listening as Michael referred to me in the vilest of terms. At that point, I knew I needed a witness, so I quietly exited the back door of my department, found Debbie Snowton sitting in her office, and asked her to follow me and listen to what was being said because I needed a witness. As we quietly entered the back door to the Student Finance department and got closer to Michael's cubicle, he was still on the phone ranting about me. "Fuck that Black bitch! I can't stand her ass! She should've been fired by now! I can't believe she's making us work over-time!"

> *I am extremely upset by Michael's conversation and demand to know if there is any truth to his statement that I was supposed to be fired by now.*
>
> *Ebony*

The next day, I received a response from Dr. Taylor and noticed she had removed Debbie Snowton from the email string. When I read her response it, quite frankly, surprised me.

> *From: Taylor, Karen*
> *Sent: Tuesday, August 01, 2017 9:19 AM*
> *To: Ardoin, Ebony*
> *Cc: MacDougal, Logan; Clayton, Travis; Brice, Charlotte*
> *Subject: FW: This is Ebony Ardoin Writing to You from Debbie Snowton's Computer*
>
> *Ebony,*
>
> *Thank you for sharing this with us. I have already discussed this with Corporate HR, and you can rest assured this will be handled with diligence and the sense of urgency it deserves.*
>
> *I'm so sorry this happened to you, Ebony, and I'm here for you. Let me know if there's anything I can do.*
>
> *Karen*

"You're here for me?" I said out loud, as I read her email. "Yeah, I believe that like I believe in a zombie apocalypse."

After reading Dr. Taylor's email, I was surprised by how quickly she turned her back on Michael and threw him to the Corporate wolves after they had been as thick as thieves for so long. And I was equally as shocked when I read her apology because it was the first time she ever apologized to me for anything, even though it was as fake as the ruse she created to have me falsely investigated for harassing Michael.

126

But even as Dr. Taylor tried to rewrite the past and play nice with me in an attempt to navigate through the firestorm she had unexpectedly found herself in, I'm sure she still believed that with a little time a patience, she would find her way out with her reputation and job still intact…or so she thought.

CHAPTER 15

From Victim to Victor

The next morning, Gabrielle took Mom to her chemo appointment so that I could work at the Temple campus and give Travis Clayton, the National Director of Human Resources, the information he needed to write the Performance Improvement Plan (PIP) that I was going to deliver to Michael. The fact that Travis was required to write the PIP was interesting to me, because normally the employee's manager was responsible for writing it. I assumed that Corporate was now sensitive to everything I had been through, and didn't want to add anything else to my plate.

Later that afternoon, I received the scathing PIP that Travis prepared. So, I called Michael to my office. When he walked in, and saw Dr. Taylor sitting in the chair in front of my desk, the look on his face was priceless. And when he sat down next to Dr. Taylor, and realized that Travis Clayton, the National Director of Human Resources, was on speaker phone, he crossed his arms as Dr. Taylor got up and closed the door.

"What's going on?" He asked, narrowing his eyes at me.

"Last night, after you thought I had left, you engaged in a highly inappropriate phone conversation with a coworker," I said. "During your conversation, you called me a Black bitch, and used the vilest of terms to describe your feelings about me."

Michael turned beet red as I provided him with a copy of the PIP. And as I read each section aloud, he kept turning to Dr. Taylor waiting for her to jump in and provide a shield of protection. He became more agitated when he discovered that the PIP not only contained a full recap of the expletives he used during his phone conversation, but it also incorporated his other behavioral issues including disappearing for extended lengths of time, rolling his eyes when I spoke, challenging my authority, failing to complete his work, and arguing with me as he questioned my decisions. It was at that moment that Michael realized it was his job, not mine, that was in jeopardy, because the tides had turned in my favor, and Dr. Taylor left him to sink or swim.

"This isn't fair! This is a bunch of B.S." He screamed, "I was told you were being fired and I was gonna be director!"

"Who told you I was being fired?" I asked.

Dr. Taylor quickly jumped in to shut Michael up.

"We're here to help you, Michael, but if you don't change your attitude, things can go from bad to worse really quick."

Dr. Taylor's warning to Michael worked like a charm. So, he sat silently with tears running down his face as I continued.

"Moving forward," I said. "I expect you to discontinue the behaviors we discussed, to conduct yourself with professionalism at all times, and to share any questions or concerns you have related to your job with me. Additionally, I will meet with you once a week to assess your progress, and want you to keep in mind that failure to meet the conditions outlined in this PIP will result in disciplinary action which could include termination of your employment. Do you have any questions?"

"No, Ms. Ebony," he replied, in between sniffles.

Afterwards, Michael, Dr. Taylor, and I signed two copies of the PIP, and I gave one to Michael for his records. Then, Michael and Dr. Taylor left my office.

The next morning, something happened that sent a shock wave across the entire Temple campus. A tall, well-groomed man with a commanding presence walked through the campus doors wearing a tailored black suit and looking like a secret service agent. He had an earpiece in one ear, a briefcase in hand, and a stern look on his face that matched his serious demeanor. And as the whispers on campus began about who he could be, one thing everyone agreed on--he was obviously someone very important.

"I'm looking for Ebony Ardoin," he sternly said to the receptionist.

"Can I get your name, sir?" The receptionist asked.

"Rick Kashinsky. I'm the CCO at Corporate."

"Okay, sir. I'll let her know you're here," the receptionist replied.

When the receptionist called me and told me who was in the lobby, a sick feeling came over me.

Why on earth is the Chief Compliance Officer here to see me? I thought to myself. *That doesn't make any sense.*

Reluctantly, I went to the lobby to greet him.

"Hi, I'm Ebony," I said, introducing myself as we shook hands.

"Nice to meet you, Ebony," he replied, with a strong, deep voice. "We need to talk."

Then, he followed me as I walked across the lobby towards the Student Finance department as the rumors on campus began to swirl.

When we were in my office behind closed doors, he sat down in the chair in front of my desk.

"When Charlotte received your discrimination complaint," he said, "she called a meeting with every executive at Corporate and gave everyone a copy as she read it aloud. Then each person was given a section to investigate, and we've been doing that for the last two months."

"Wow. That's good to know," I replied. "No one responded to my emails, so I assumed nothing was being done."

"The portion of the investigation surrounding your discrimination complaint is complete and the findings will be forthcoming," he said. "The last part of the investigation surrounds allegations of misconduct and unethical behavior made against you by Dr. Taylor."

Then Rick said that, according to Dr. Taylor, Michael discovered that I had changed the packaging statuses of numerous students from incomplete to complete, without the required documentation, to boost my team's packaging rates, and make it appear that my department was performing at a higher level than other campuses. And when he reported my unethical behavior and misconduct to Logan, I harassed and threatened him to the point of resigning.

"That's a lie," I said, trying not to get choked up. "I worked very hard to develop solid processes that improved student finance operations, including the speed at which we complete packages. And I never harassed Michael or anyone. Dr. Taylor, Logan, and Michael created a ruse to make it appear that I had harassed Michael because they needed a reason to fire me."

130

Then, Rick said that Dr. Taylor provided Corporate with the names of seven students whose packaging statuses were unethically changed from incomplete to complete as proof of my misconduct.

"We want to give you a chance to respond to the allegations," he said. "So, you have thirty days."

"I'll do better than respond," I said, with confidence. "I'll prove to you right here, right now that I'm innocent."

Then, I asked Rick to bring his chair around to my side of the desk and observe, as I reviewed the packaging activities for each student in question. One by one, I examined each student's record in the student database, followed the audit trail showing all entries made and by whom, and read the detailed notes I trained my team to enter providing an explanation for every action taken. Two hours and two cups of coffee later, I had successfully proved that all seven allegations made against me were completely false.

"Dr. Taylor also alleged that you developed and implemented processes that were flawed and put the campus at risk for future compliance issues," Rick said. "But we received information from Aaron Burns, the CSFO at Corporate, that proved otherwise."

After instructing me to email him my process documentation, he informed me that someone at Corporate would be in touch to discuss next steps, and then he left.

As I sat in my office thinking about everything Rick had shared with me, I wasn't the least bit surprised when I learned of Dr. Taylor's underhanded attempt to deflect Corporate's attention from the systemic racism I had reported.

Later that afternoon, mom's doctor called my sister Gabrielle and requested to meet with us. The next day, I took off from work, and me, Gabrielle, and Mom went to the cancer center. As we waited for the doctor to arrive, all three of us were on edge and praying that he was going to give us good news.

Ten minutes later, the doctor arrived and sat down at his desk.

"We've done everything we can, Babette," he said, with sorrow in his eyes. "The chemo isn't working, and I'm afraid there isn't anything else we can do."

When I heard the doctor say we had reached the end of the road in mom's cancer treatment, I cried so hard my head and chest hurt as I gripped mom's hand, and refused to let her go. Gabrielle was crying hysterically, too, as she gripped mom's other hand so tight it almost cut off her circulation, and tried to convince the doctor that he had it all wrong, that there were more options he had for saving mom's life he needed to explore.

As Gabrielle and I sprinted across the thin line from hope to denial, Mom sat in a state of shock, and for the first few minutes she was as still as stone. She didn't cry. She didn't move. She didn't speak. She just stared at the decorative clock sitting on her doctor's desk, as if it was somehow mocking her, that it knew her time was up, and she was going to die.

Then, mom's emotions caught up with the rest of ours, as tear after precious tear rolled down her face.

"How long do I have?" Mom quietly asked, with eyes full of sadness.

"I don't want to put a time limit on your life, Babette," the doctor replied. "Let's focus on getting you setup with in-home hospice, and making you as comfortable as possible in your own surroundings."

"Please," Mom pleaded. "Just give it to me straight. How long before I die?"

After Mom asked her question, the room was silent. There was no sound, except the ticking of the decorative clock on her doctor's desk, and the whispering wind coming through the window.

Then, mom's doctor sighed, and answered the question that had been on mom's mind since he gave us the devastating news.

"About one to two months," he sadly said.

Mom thanked her doctor for his candor, and then cried like she's never cried before, as we called the rest of our relatives and gave them the heartbreaking news. Then, we took Mom home.

"Girls, promise me I will not be cremated," Mom said, as we helped her get into her pajamas and climb into bed. "I want to be buried, and I want to wear my white suit. You know, the one I wore to the pastor's anniversary, with my white hat."

"Okay, mom," Gabrielle and I said, as we both climbed into her bed and laid with her, hugging her tight.

Over the next two days, I was inconsolable and found myself pulling weeds in my backyard until I collapsed from exhaustion. I pulled weeds for hours, big ones and little ones early in the morning and late at night, as I tried to cope with the fact that Mom was going to die. Day after day I pulled those weeds, until my fingers cramped and, in some cases, bled.

When I returned to work the following morning, Dr. Gershon, the CEO of the Daebrun division, sent an all-staff email that hit the Temple campus with the force of a magnitude 6.0 earthquake.

From: Gershon, Harry
Sent: Monday, August 07, 2017 10:01 AM
To: @DAEBRUN-TEM Staff
Subject: Organizational Announcement

Colleagues,

Please be advised that Dr. Karen Taylor (Chancellor), Logan MacDougal (Vice President of Finance), and Michael Sullivan (Student Finance Advisor) are no longer with our organization, effective immediately. We wish them the best of luck as they pursue future endeavors.

Moving forward, please direct all questions and issues related to Temple campus operations to Amanda Ross, Chancellor at the Austin campus, who will serve as acting Chancellor for Temple until further notice.

With respect,

Harry Gershon, Ph.D., CEO

As news of the unexpected departures of Dr. Taylor, Logan, and Michael reverberated through the halls like aftershocks, I was sitting in my office feeling emotionally numb. Don't get me wrong, I was thrilled that their racism had finally caught up with them, and that they were officially gone, but after everything they put me through, the abuse I suffered, the humiliation I endured, and the terror I felt as they harshly tried to take away my livelihood as Mom was dying from cancer, sending a mere email announcement to end my long and horrific journey seemed anticlimactic. I guess, in some way, I wanted Corporate to shoot them or stab them. Stab them or shoot them.

The next day, I received a call from my attorney.

"Daebrun has requested to use mediation to settle the discrimination complaints with you, Latoya and Christine," she said. "Because you're the only one who filed a complaint with the State of Texas, they want to resolve your issues first, so your complaint with the state can be withdrawn."

When I heard this news, I breathed a long sigh of relief because I knew it was only a matter of time before my case was settled, and my horrific journey working for Daebrun would be a thing of the past.

"My assistant will email you the date, time and location, and I'll overnight the mediation brief to you later this week," she continued.

Three days later, I received the mediation brief that my attorney prepared and had also sent to Corporate. It included an opening statement containing a summary of events and stating that I was seeking four hundred thousand dollars to settle my racial discrimination claims against Daebrun.

There was a Factual Background section that detailed every discriminatory event, in chronological order, that had occurred since the day I was hired as a Daebrun employee in 2012.

There was a section that covered the weaknesses of Daebrun's defense against my claims, which included long-term evidence of systemic racism in the form of racial epithets used in reference to Black employees, pay inequality for Black employees, and preferential treatment of White employees.

There was a section that covered the perceived weaknesses of my claims against Daebrun, which included the two promotions I received over the course of five-years, the argument that the National Director of Student Finance position was eliminated for legitimate business reasons, and the argument that the emotional distress I suffered resulting in my medical leave of absence had more to do with the stress I was under due to mom's cancer diagnosis and less to do with the conditions at work.

And lastly, there was a section on the monetary compensation that I could be awarded by a jury, which my attorney estimated could be double the amount I was seeking, for lost income, lost benefits, emotional distress, attorney fees and costs, and punitive damages if a court date was established and my case went to trial. It also included unspecified damages to Daebrun's reputation if news of the systemic racism in their organization became public.

The following week, my attorney and I drove to the mediation firm located about twenty minutes away from my attorney's law office. When we arrived, we were greeted by the mediator who escorted us to a conference room and instructed us to have a seat at the conference table where Dr. Gershon, the CEO of the Daebrun division, and Corporate's Legal Counsel were sitting. Then, the proceedings began.

First, the mediator introduced everyone, explained the steps in the mediation process, and laid down some ground rules like don't interrupt when someone is speaking, and to be respectful at all times. Then, she explained that her role in the mediation process was to facilitate dialogue between both parties that moved us closer to a settlement agreement.

Next, I was given the opportunity to describe everything that had happened to me over the course of my five-year tenure at Daebrun. My emotions were raw as I relived every painful moment over a two-hour period, and tearfully described how the American dream, the dream that made me believe I could have the same opportunities at Daebrun that were afforded to White employees, became a living nightmare because I was Black. I described how Ms. Kelly treated me like I was a wild horse she was determined and eager to tame. How she humiliated me in meetings, degraded and dehumanized me with threats and fear, took away my job duties, called me Agony constantly, and threatened me repeatedly during my first year of employment. And how she used my Blackness as a marketing tool to increase minority enrollments at Daebrun during my second year, and verbally attacked me and told me that I committed career suicide after I filed the anonymous discrimination complaint against Malcolm Webb during my third year.

Then, I described how Malcolm mercilessly retaliated against me by changing the work I completed and riddling it with errors to make it appear I was incompetent and put my job at risk, verbally abused me in front of coworkers, called me Darky in private, pressured me to resign, made me work more late shifts than anyone else, and tampered with my financial aid, as well as my sister's financial aid, after we became students at Daebrun creating financial hardships for us. And how he continued his retaliation, even after being fired for racial discrimination, by filing multiple fake anonymous discrimination complaints against me, putting me in a position of constantly having to defend myself.

Next, I described how Kyle Charron set me up for failure after I was promoted to Director of Student Finance and harassed me for months, then secretly traveled to the Temple campus where he called me a snake in the grass, threatened to chop my head off with a shovel, and said, "You're full of so much shit your skin is brown!"

But it wasn't until I started describing the harassment and abuse that I suffered during my fourth and fifth years under Dr. Taylor's leadership that I really broke down and started to sob. I described how Dr. Taylor referred to my braids as worms, said I didn't sound Black, used mom's terminal cancer diagnosis as the spark to target me at my most vulnerable moment, and set her plan in motion to destroy my reputation, derail my career, take away my livelihood when I needed it most, and replace me with my White subordinate, not because he was more qualified, but because he was White. I explained how she denied me the authority of my position, prevented me from performing the duties associated with my job, assigned my duties to my White subordinate to carry out, actively blocked promotion opportunities and opportunities I had for growth, conspired with other White leaders and my White employee to have me falsely investigated for harassment, and fostered a work environment that was so hostile that after only six months had passed, I was completely stripped of all dignity, confidence, and strength, and suffered a mental breakdown.

After I was finished telling my story, the room was silent for several minutes and when I glanced at Dr. Gershon staring at me from across the table, I saw a tear in his eye.

"Ebony, I know you've been through a lot," he said. "And it's my understanding you want to end your employment. Correct?"

"Yes." I replied.

"Through your courage, you've brought awareness to the racial divide in our organization, but if we're going to fix it, we need your help. So, I'm here to ask you not to resign."

"Thank you, but there's absolutely no way I can continue working at the Temple campus."

Then, Dr. Gershon made me an offer I found hard to refuse. He offered to transfer me back to the Austin campus to be closer to mom, promote me to the National Director of Student Finance position I was promised, increase my salary from sixty-six thousand dollars a year to eighty-six thousand a year, provide diversity training to the employees at all campuses in the Daebrun division, create a Diversity Committee I would help lead, give me four weeks of paid vacation to give me time to rest and be with mom, and pay me two hundred thousand dollars, plus attorney fees and costs, for my emotional distress and to settle the discrimination complaint I filed with the State of Texas.

Afterwards, I was given some privacy to consult with my attorney. And after weighing the pros and cons, and realizing that the settlement amount was not subject to federal tax, I decided to accept his offer because it enabled me to work in the same city where I lived and could be closer to mom, allowed me to continue the career I worked so hard to build with my medical, dental, 401K and tuition reimbursement benefits still intact, and provided me with a six-figure lump sum payment for my emotional distress now, instead of waiting years for the State of Texas to complete its investigation, issue a Right to Sue letter, and for a court date to be established for trial.

On my way home, I called to check on mom. "Child, I was layin' here on pins and needles waitin' for ya call," she said in a weak voice. "How did it go?"

"It went better than I ever imagined, mom," I replied.

After giving Mom all the details about what happened and what I received to settle my claims, Mom was elated.

"Thank God I'm alive to see you win this battle, honey!" Mom exclaimed, excitedly. "I told ya God has a way of workin' things out. All ya gotta do is believe."

The next day, my employee Marisol was promoted to the Director of Student Finance at the Temple campus, and I spent the day training her on everything she needed to know and helping her interview candidates to replace her two open positions.

One day later, my attorney received the Settlement Agreement and Release of Claims that was prepared by Corporate's Legal Counsel, and emailed it to me, to read and sign, along with a W-9 form for tax reporting purposes. And as a read the sections of the settlement agreement requiring confidentiality and nondisclosure, I realized at that moment that the compensation, and everything else, that Dr. Gershon offered me to settle my discrimination claims, was actually different forms of hush money, given to me to hide the systemic racism at Daebrun, and guarantee my silence.

As I drove away from the Temple campus with my personal belongings in my trunk, and thanked God for transforming me from the racial discrimination victim I once was to a racial discrimination victor, I looked forward to continuing my career at the Austin campus with a different staff, different coworkers, and a fresh start. And I was confident my journey would be better tomorrow than it was yesterday, optimistic that the racial divide, with my help, would finally be closed, and relieved that my battles against systemic racism at Daebrun had finally come to an end...or so I thought.